Hydroponic
Home Food Gardens

Hydroponic Home Food Gardens

By Howard M. Resh

Formerly, University of British Columbia
Author of Hydroponic Food Production
International Consultant, Hydroponic Gardening and Farming

Published by
Woodbridge Press / *Santa Barbara, CA 93160*

1994

Published by

Woodbridge Press Publishing Company
Post Office Box 209
Santa Barbara, California 93102

Distributed simultaneously in the United States and Canada

Printed in the United States of America

Library of Congress Cataloging-in-Publication Data:

Resh, Howard M.
    Hydroponic home food gardens / Howard M. Resh
      p. cm.
    Includes bibliographical references.
    Includes index.
    ISBN 0-88007-178-8 : $12.95
      1. Hydroponics. 2. Food crops. I. Title.
SB126.5. R48   1990   90-12143
635'.0485—dc20   CIP

Contents

INTRODUCTION

Hydroponic Gardening: Less Care, More Results

This book will help you to produce your own pesticide-free, clean, nutritious vegetables and fruits.

And you can do this without the usual struggle with slugs, cutworms, nematodes, or other soil-borne pests.

You need not weed or hoe.

You do not have to dig up your garden patch every spring and add unknown quantities of lime and other fertilizers in an effort to increase the soil fertility.

Even if you have no garden plot at all, but still enjoy the flavor of freshly-picked vegetables and fruits, you can grow them hydroponically in a very small space, indoors or out.

Modern hydroponic methods—using a neutral growing medium instead of soil—will produce an abundant supply of the most desirable fresh foods such as lettuce, spinach, chard, tomatoes, peppers, cucumbers, and more.

And all these wonderful foods will be clean, nutritious, free of unknown poisons, and have real backyard-grown flavor!

You should experience greater yields per square foot in crops grown hydroponically than in traditional gardening. If sufficient sunlight is available, plants can be spaced closer together in a soilless system in comparison with soil culture. A hydroponic system, properly managed, should produce at least a 20-25 percent increase in yields of tomatoes, cucumbers, peppers, and lettuce, for example.

Because hydroponics lends itself to automation, a great deal less work is required. And it is nice to know that, if you do use a simple automated system, you can take a vacation for several weeks without worrying about whether your plants are being watered and fed!

And you can grow beautiful vegetables, and fruits, too, in very small spaces, either inside or outdoors.

Indoor units, with supplementary artificial light, or placed on window sills, balconies, decks, or in patios can be amazingly productive.

On a larger scale, a modest backyard greenhouse can produce enough vegetables and fruits not only for your family but also for relatives, friends, and neighbors—if you wish!

A hydroponic garden may be small, simple, and inexpensive or it may be larger, elaborate, and fully automated, as is often the case with a garden created in a small backyard greenhouse.

In addition to its productivity, a home hydroponic garden can give you carefree relaxation and the rewards of achievement and satisfaction.

This book will describe various kinds of home hydroponic systems you can use for both small and large-scale gardens or backyard greenhouses.

It will give you especially valuable information on plant care as well as the conditions plants need for sound growth and nutrition.

Some chapters describe the essential nutrient elements found in plants, and where those elements come from, as well as the uses, characteristics, and treatment of soilless media suitable for hydroponic gardening.

You will learn about ready-made nutrient preparations you can buy, or you can make up your own from the nutrient formulations given here for specific plants in your home garden.

Seven basic hydroponic systems are described in detail so that you may choose the best one for your garden, indoors or outdoors, small or large, manual or automated.

If you have the space and wish to use it, a backyard greenhouse may be your choice. Details on building such a greenhouse are given as well as instructions for constructing any of the hydro-ponic systems for your backyard greenhouse.

Guidelines are presented for selecting the most useful plant varieties, seeding, plant spacing, training, pruning, and pollinat-ing; techniques that will assure you of successful gardening.

An awareness of potential plant pests and diseases described here will assist you in avoiding and/or controlling them with biological agents, soaps, and safe insecticides.

An Appendix and Bibliography provide sources of supplies, hydroponic systems, equipment, seeds, as well as lists of pe-riodicals and references for further reading on horticulture and hydroponics.

Hydroponics:
Ancient and Modern

The word "hydroponics," first used in the early 1930's, was derived from two Greek words meaning "water-working." It is often defined as the science of growing plants without soil. Perhaps a better term would be "soilless culture," since this would encompass all the various methods of "growing without soil."

Hydroponics itself, more technically, would be soilless culture using water as a growing medium, which is a more limited definition than I use in this book. Other terms describing soilless culture are nutriculture and hydroculture.

All of these terms have come to be included in our present use of the word "hydroponics." All of them signify the use of: 1) a soilless medium like gravel or vermiculite in which plants can grow, and 2) water, containing essential plant nutrients—fertilizers, if you will—in solution, dispersed throughout the growing medium, delivering nutrients to the plant roots. (One slight variant is "aeroponics," in which plant roots are suspended in a chamber and supplied with water and nutrients in the form of mist.)

Ancient Science

Regardless of the terminology and the techniques that have developed over the past 50 years or so, the science of growing plants without soil is much older. It existed in the floating gardens of the Aztecs of Mexico, and Egyptian hieroglyphic records describe the growing of plants in water. Even the hanging gardens of Babylon may be thought of as hydroponic gardens.

Beginning in the 1600's, scientists conducted experiments to determine what substances plants take from water and soil. Work was continued by chemists during the 18th and 19th centuries to demonstrate that plants require certain basic elements provided by air, water, and soil. By the late 1800's, horticultural scientists were able to grow plants successfully in nothing more than a water solution containing the various minerals that plants require for growth and development.

This knowledge was limited to laboratory experiments until the 1930's, when W. F. Gericke developed the principles in a commercially successful way.

In the early 1940's, in order to feed troops on isolated, nonarable islands in the Pacific, the United States Army established large hydroponic farms.

With postwar development of new plastic products and the expansion of the greenhouse industry in proximity to large city markets, year-round intensive cropping in greenhouse soils rapidly depleted them of nutrients. Poor soil composition, structure, and nutrition reduced yields. Further complications of pests and diseases pressured growers to find an alternative method.

No Need for Great Expense

They found that the new plastics eliminated the need for the expensive concrete beds and tanks formerly used in hydroponic systems. Soilless culture for greenhouse crops became widely accepted as a new technology to overcome problems of growing crops in the soil. (Growers used various materials—sawdust, peat, pumice, rice hulls, vermiculite, perlite, sand, and gravel as a substitute for soil.)

Regrettably, this "newly developed" technology of hydroponics became, especially during the 1960's, the newest "get-rich-quick" scheme of many overly enthusiastic promoters. Nevertheless, it has continued advancing technically and is now accountable for producing more than 90–95 percent of all greenhouse-grown vegetables, flowers, and ornamentals.

This highly developed science can easily and productively be adapted to small-scale home gardening.

Although some references in this book are to specific soilless systems as used in commercial operations, the emphasis is on a simplified, smaller-scale use by the gardening enthusiast.

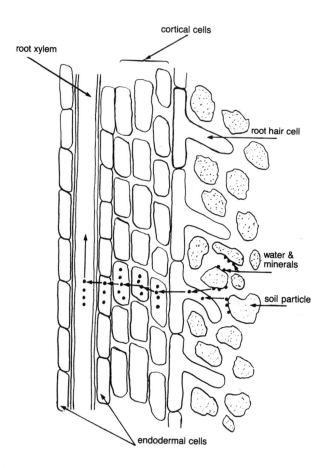

Figure 1. Water and mineral absorption by plant roots. Longitudinal section of root tip in root hair zone.

Life and Growth of Plants

This feature explains the basic plant life processes of water and mineral uptake, plant nutrition, manufacture of plant foods (photosynthesis), and the functions of roots and shoots.

When I talk with people about "hydroponics," they often remark, "Oh, that's how you grow plants without any soil or light." My reply is, "Hydroponics is only a method of growing *without soil*. All other horticultural needs of plants are the same as if they were grown in soil."

You can be more successful in growing plants hydroponically if you have an understanding of how plants grow and develop.

Plants take carbon dioxide (CO_2) from the air.

They require water as a medium for obtaining minerals essential for growth and development.

Water serves as a cooling substance during evapotranspiration (loss of water from the plant by evaporation and transpiration). Water transports essential elements to food manufacturing sites in the leaves during photosynthesis and conducts photosynthates (the products of photosynthesis) and hormones throughout the plant to produce growth.

If you understand the basic requirements and functions of plants, you can better care for them by providing the environmental conditions favorable to healthy plant growth.

Basic Life Processes

Plant survival depends on the basic life processes of absorption of water and food (nutrition), transportation of water and foods throughout the plant (translocation), making of foods by photosynthesis, the breaking down of foods using energy to drive the chemical changes (respiration) needed in cell division and multiplication for growth, reproduction, and repair.

The series of cellular functions involving energy for life and growth of plants is metabolism. Respiration involves chemical

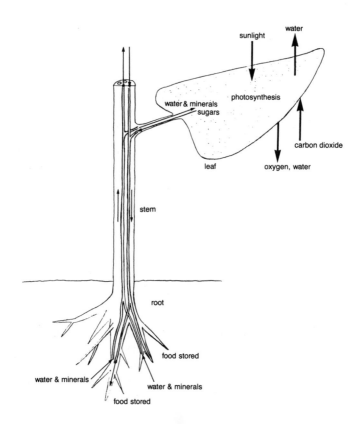

Figure 2. Water, mineral, and photosynthate movement within the plant.

reactions that release the energy of plant food for use by cells. This released energy is used in all the life processes.

The Root System

The most important function of the root is to absorb water and minerals. It also provides plant support and contact with soil (or artificial medium) particles. Minerals held by the "soil" particles are exchanged with the surrounding soil-water solution. This soil-water solution carries and transfers minerals essential for plant growth to the root surface, where absorption takes place (fig. 1).

The *essential elements,* those mineral elements which must be present within the plant to enable it to grow and develop are nitrogen (N), phosphorus (P), potassium (K), magnesium (Mg), calcium (Ca), sulfur (S), iron (Fe), manganese (Mn), boron (B), copper (Cu), zinc (Zn), molybdenum (Mo), and chlorine (Cl). The letters in the parentheses are the chemical symbols for each element. In addition, hydrogen (H), oxygen (O_2) and carbon (C) are essential elements—available from the air and water. These latter three and the first six elements mentioned above (H, O_2, C, N, P, K, Mg, Ca, and S) are required in relatively large quantities and hence are called *macroelements,* while the others (Fe, Mn, B, Cu, Zn, Mo, and Cl), required in relatively small amounts, are termed *microelements.*

In natural soil these elements come from leaching of rocks and minerals and from decomposition of organic matter. Often soils are deficient in a number of these elements and optimum plant growth is restricted.

In a hydroponic system we provide the essential elements by the addition of fertilizer salts to the water. This *nutrient solution,* in hydroponics, is the equivalent of the natural soil-water solution in conventional gardening.

Minerals and water are absorbed by the *root hairs* at the tips of roots. Water and mineral *ions* (electrically charged atoms or groups of atoms) move into the plant root via the interconnecting cell walls and intercellular spaces or through a system of interconnected protoplasm of the cells.

To enter the vascular system of the plant, minerals and water must move through a layer of cells (endodermal cells) which regulates their movement according to the plant needs, in response to environmental conditions. Clearly then, if environmental conditions are not favorable to *plant uptake of water and minerals,* growth will be sub-optimal.

Water and minerals move up the roots to the stem and leaves via the conducting (xylem) tissue. Foods manufactured in the leaves (photosynthates) are generally transported downwards to locations of useage in the plant or to storage sites such as fruits, stems, or roots via the phloem-conducting tissues (fig. 2). The *xylem* and *phloem* make up the vascular tissue (veins).

The Shoot System

The shoot system consists of stems and leaves. The stem provides framework for the plant and gives leaves favorable exposure to light. The vascular tissues conduct water and minerals in the xylem (conducting tissue) upward from the roots to the leaves where photosynthesis takes place. Photosynthates move from the manufacture source to other plant parts via the phloem of the vascular tissue. Stems also store food and bear reproductive structures such as flowers and fruit.

The points where leaves or side branches are attached to the stem are termed *nodes,* while the lengths between them are *internodes.* In the angles where leaves are attached to stems, buds develop which can produce side shoots. In most vegetable crops such as tomatoes, cucumbers, and peppers, these side shoots must be removed in order to train the plant vertically. Training is discussed in more detail in Chapter 4.

Leaves are the site of *photosynthesis* (fig. 3). Photosynthesis is the process whereby light energy is absorbed by the chlorophyll molecules (green pigment of leaves). It combines the essential elements of the water solution with the carbon, oxygen, and hydrogen from the air and water to form photosynthates (simple sugars). For those readers interested in the chemistry, a simplified equation for this reaction is:

$$\text{sunlight} + 12H_2O + 6CO_2 \xrightarrow[\text{energy}]{\text{light}} 6O_2 + C_6H_{12}O_6 + 6H_2O$$

$$\text{(water)} \quad \text{(carbon dioxide)} \qquad \text{(oxygen)} \quad \text{(sugars)} \quad \text{(water)}$$

Chloroplasts, small green bodies in leaf cells, contain chlorophyll (green pigment). The chlorophyll acts as a solar energy collector and is involved in trapping solar energy needed in the conversion of water and carbon dioxide into simple sugars during photosynthesis. This photosynthetic reaction is the basis for all higher plant life.

The photosynthates, together with water, are transported to fruits and storage organs which, in food crops, are edible to man. The better the environmental conditions for the plant, the more photosynthates are manufactured, enabling the plant to produce higher fruit yields. (A secondary benefit to man from photosynthesis is the removal of carbon dioxide from air and the release of oxygen into the atmosphere.)

During transpiration, plant leaves lose over 95 percent of the water taken up by roots. This cools the plant leaves and surrounding atmosphere. It is also the driving force for the movement of water and minerals from the roots to the leaves. Movement of water out of leaves takes place mostly on the leaf undersides via the stomates (small pores).

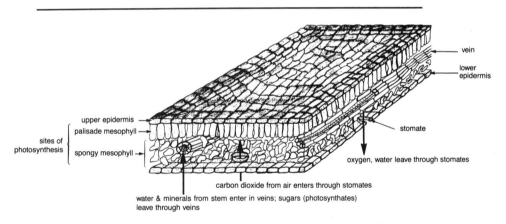

Figure 3. Leaf structure with movement of CO_2, O_2 and water and the site of photosynthesis.

CHAPTER 1 | # Choosing the Best Hydroponic System for Your Home Garden

In this chapter we discuss how to choose the right hydroponic system for you—based on your garden size, the type of construction, how much automation you may decide to use, and, of course, your budget.

You will see how, if you wish, you can grow plants without any solid medium at all, in straight water culture, or in what is called nutrient film technique (NFT).

More likely, you will want to make use of the information here about commercially available, sterile, synthetic media such as rockwool, perlite, or vermiculite, into which plants are inserted and through which a nutrient solution is circulated to nourish the plants.

Alternatively, we also discuss the use of a natural medium such as sand, sawdust, peat, or gravel.

Do-it-yourself methods, the materials required, and the most suitable systems for growing specific crops are described.

Many illustrations make it easy to understand what your choices are and the details of how to make your hydroponic garden a reality.

Water Culture

In straight water-culture hydroponics, plants are secured so that roots are bathed in water in which the necessary fertilizer salts (the nutrients) have been dissolved.

Although most plants can be grown by water culture, if adequate oxygenation is provided in the nutrient solution, the leafy vegetables like lettuce, spinach, chard, and herbs do best.

Water-culture systems are "recirculated," or closed, in that the nutrient solution passes through the plant roots in the beds and then drains back to the solution tank or reservoir. Normally, the solution is circulated continuously with a pump.

In a floating, or "raceway," system the growing bed itself is also the nutrient solution tank. In this case, especially, oxygenation of the solution is imperative for success. An aquarium pump attached to a perforated tube at the bottom of the bed (which, as stated, is also the nutrient solution tank) will supply adequate oxygen to plant roots (fig. 4). The pump should operate continuously.

Alternatively, the growing bed or beds may be separated from the nutrient reservoir. This will permit somewhat larger gardens. Plastic piping (PVC) conducts the solution from the nutrient reservoir to the bed inlet, driven by a pump (fig. 5). The flow of each inlet into the bed is regulated by a gate valve. A return line from the opposite end of the bed carries the solution back to the tank, or reservoir. (The outlet for the return line should be about 2 inches below the top edge of the bed so that the solution is maintained at that level.) Pipe of 1½-inch diameter should be used.

These "overflow" pipes actually join to a common 2-inch diameter return line which conducts the nutrient solution back to the tank. The inlet valves must be opened sufficiently to keep the solution flowing but not so much as to exceed the overflow rate.

In a larger system containing more plants, water is rapidly used up and must be replenished in the solution reservoir. This is easily controlled by a float value such as a toilet float-valve assembly, which stops the flow of water when it reaches a set level.

A common waste line connected to each bed allows changing of the solution, after a crop in one bed, without interfering with

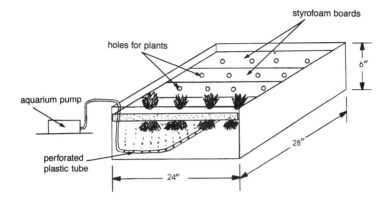

Figure 4. A small-scale raceway water culture system.

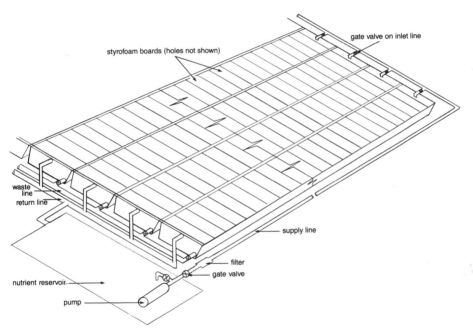

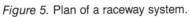

Figure 5. Plan of a raceway system.

Figure 6. A raceway system using extruded plastic beds with styrofoam boards. *Courtesy of Hoppmann Hydroponics, Waverly, Florida.*

Figure 7. Mature lettuce (32 days after transplanting). Note the four plants per styrofoam board with roots hanging below. *Courtesy of Hoppmann Hydroponics, Waverly, Florida.*

the plants growing in adjacent beds. A 1½-inch diameter pipe is secured to the bottom edge of each bed and joined to a common 2-inch diameter waste line. A gate value at the outlet is opened to drain a bed, and the solution is allowed to drain outside to waste.

This type of system would be appropriate for a backyard hydroponic garden, whereas the smaller, combined tray-on-tank system mentioned above would be more suitable for indoor units.

Growing beds for a greenhouse garden should be the length of the greenhouse by 2 feet (60 cm) wide by 6–8 inches (15–20 cm) deep. They may be constructed of fiberglass, or wood lined with 20-mil-thick vinyl. Smaller indoor units may be made from a plastic tote bin such as those used in restaurants.

The plants are grown on floating styrofoam boards 1 inch (2.5 cm) thick by 7 inches (18 cm) wide with a length slightly less than the width of the bed to allow free movement of the boards along the bed (figs. 6, 7). The high density, blue-colored "roof-mate" product used as insulation in house construction is ideal material for the boards.

One-inch diameter holes are drilled through the boards at correct spacing for the crop grown. Generally, for lettuce, spinach, and herbs, this would be approximately 7 inches (18 cm) apart in each board. For boards 23–24 inches (60 cm) in length, four plants would fit into each one. A small, thick paper or plastic support is cut to cover each hole and support the plant seedling.

Disinfect the boards and beds with a 10 percent chlorine bleach solution between crops. Rinse the boards with raw water and allow them to dry before using them on the next crop. Change the nutrient solution only between crops, generally every 30–35 days.

Sow seeds in either a flat, using a vegetable plug (peat-vermiculite) mix, or directly into rockwood cubes (fig. 8). Do not use peat pellets as they become excessively saturated in the beds, resulting in an oxygen deficit which promotes soft rot in the crown of the plants.

Transplant the seedlings to the beds 10–14 days after sowing (fig. 9). Providing the seedlings with cool-white fluorescent lighting (about one foot above the plants) will produce stalky plants.

The seedlings should have at least four true leaves before transplanting. With spinach and slower growing herbs, seedlings may have to be in excess of three weeks old before transplanting.

Figure 8. Lettuce seedlings from 7 to 10 days old sown in flats with vegetable plug mix medium. Trays are set on a capillary matting in small beds to obtain irrigation. *Courtesy of Hoppmann Hydroponics, Homestead, Florida.*

Figure 9. Lettuce seedling grown in plug tray ready for transplanting.

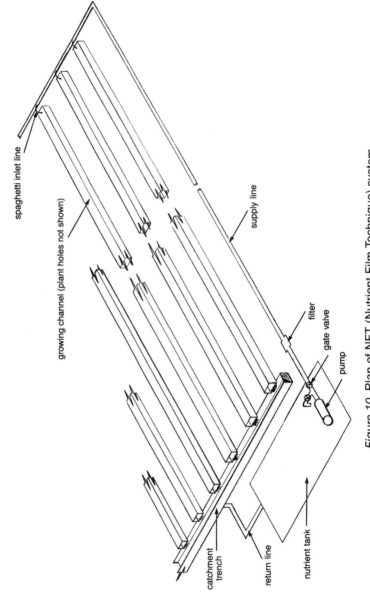

spaghetti inlet line

growing channel (plant holes not shown)

supply line

filter

gate valve

pump

catchment trench

return line

nutrient tank

Figure 10. Plan of NFT (Nutrient Film Technique) system.

Nutrient Film Technique (NFT)

A simpler method of water culture is the NFT system. This method uses small plastic channels as beds and a relatively large nutrient solution reservoir. It is a closed system, with the solution circulating continuously via a pump and plastic piping (fig. 10).

The plastic channels may be purchased (see Appendix) or the home gardener may use plastic or aluminum gutters—or 3-inch (7.5 cm) diameter PVC piping (fig. 11).

The channels are supported by a metal framework with a two percent slope back to a catchment trench positioned perpendicularly across the back ends of the growing channels (figs. 10, 12, 13). This trench can be a plastic or aluminium gutter or 3-inch PVC pipe which collects the nutrient solution from the growing channels and conducts it back to the nutrient reservoir.

The nutrient solution is pumped from the reservoir continuously via a ¾-inch diameter black polyvinyl header having "spaghetti" lines attached to the inlet end of each growing channel or trough (figs. 10, 14). The growing beds initially can be tightly spaced during early stages of plant growth and later separated as the growing plants require more area. Final spacing for lettuce would be about 7 inches (18 cm) between channels and 7 inches (18 cm) between plants within each channel row (fig. 15).

The channels have a rigid plastic cover through which holes are cut for placement of the plants (fig. 16). If seedlings are started in rockwool cubes, the holes should be cut just wide enough (about ¾-inch–1 inch) to contain the plant and rockwool cube. The depth of 1½ inches (4 cm) is sufficient for the growing channel (fig. 17).

A modification of this system is to place a series of channels on a metal A-frame (fig. 18). The channels are arranged in a spiral, like an extended spring, so that they slope about two percent all the way around (fig. 19). If the A-frame is about 6 to 7 feet (2 m) high, approximately nine runs can be supported.

To avoid oxygen deficit to the plants, a set of runs should not exceed 70 feet (21 m) in length. This is achieved by separating runs into units, each having its own inlet and outlet.

A nutrient reservoir, positioned below the frame, stores the solution. Common headers from the reservoir for inlet and outlet

Figure 11. NFT system using 2½-inch diameter PVC pipes. Note irrigation line header and individual spaghetti inlet lines to each channel. *Courtesy of Garden Patch Produce, Sarasota, Florida.*

Figure 12. Plastic gutter NFT system. Note the galvanized steel supporting frame, the ¾-inch diameter black polyethylene header pipe and emitters with spaghetti lines to each tray. Also, note yellow sticky card hanging above the crop to catch insects. *Courtesy of Gourmet Hydroponics, Lake Wales, Florida.*

Figure 13. Exit ends of gutters returning nutrient solution to a catchment trench, which takes the solution back to a reservoir. *Courtesy of Gourmet Hydroponics, Lake Wales, Florida.*

Figure 14. Plastic gutter NFT system showing inlet header, emitters and trickle feed lines to each gutter. *Courtesy of Gourmet Hydroponics, Lake Wales, Florida.*

Figure 15. Inlet end of plastic gutter NFT system. Note the young plants (about 14 days old) are close together while the older ones on the left are spaced farther apart. Spacing is accomplished by progressively moving the trays apart as the plants are harvested at the other end. *Courtesy of Gourmet Hydroponics, Lake Wales, Florida.*

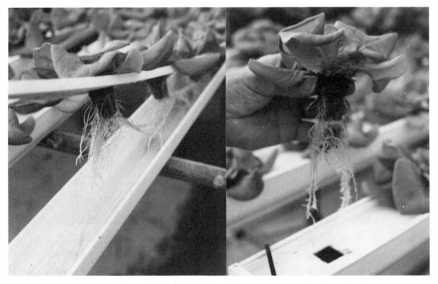

Figure 16. A rigid plastic cover supports the plants grown in rockwool cubes. *Courtesy of Gourmet Hydroponics, Lake Wales, Florida.*

Figure 17. Rockwool cube in which seedling was grown is placed into the top cover of the plastic gutter. *Courtesy of Gourmet Hydroponics, Lake Wales, Florida.*

Figure 18. A series of 2½-inch diameter PVC pipes supported on an A-frame. Lettuce seedlings are started in
mesh pots with a vermiculite or granular rockwool medium.

Figure 19. PVC channels run spirally around the metal A-frame supporting structure.

Figure 20. The nutrient reservoir is located below with a submersible pump connected to an inlet header and a common return (on right).

33

Figure 21. Double row NFT channel with semi-rigid black plastic channel and an opaque white cover supporting lettuce. An extensive root mat forms along the channel.

lines are constructed of PVC pipe. The inlet header can be ¾-inch diameter black polyethylene piping with spaghetti lines connecting each bed unit. The return header should be at least 1½-inch diameter PVC piping (fig. 20).

Several other types of NFT trays are sold by various green-house suppliers. Even if you can't find suitable trays (like some that are manufactured in Holland for commercial growers and are unavailable to the hobbyist) the designs may suggest practical ways of constructing your own.

For example, a semi-rigid black polyethylene tray for growing two rows of lettuce or leafy vegetables (fig. 21) could be constructed of wood lined with 6-mil black polyethylene sheeting. In this case, grow one row of plants instead of two per trough. The trough should be built of 1-inch by 6-inch lumber on the bottom and 1-inch by 3-inch sides. After placing the poly liner inside, fold the edges up to form a tent configuration and staple the edges between the plants. Insert small stakes through the poly across the channel between each plant to keep the poly from collapsing into the trough (fig. 22).

When transplanting the seedlings into the growing channel, place a 4-inch (10 cm)-wide strip of paper towel across the channel bottom, directly under each seedling. This will intercept the nutrient solution running down the channel and disperse it laterally to the seedling roots. The other components—inlet, return, and nutrient reservoir—are constructed in the manner described above.

A multi-channel NFT system may be constructed of corrugated metal or corrugated concrete sheets with either a vinyl or styrofoam cover (fig. 23). If metal is used, it must be coated with an epoxy resin or other waterproof sealer compound to prevent the nutrient solution from corroding the metal. Every other channel could be left unused to allow adequate spacing of 7 inches (18 cm) between rows for crops such as lettuce or spinach. The other components—inlet and header pipes, spaghetti line feeders, catchment trench, and nutrient tank—would be constructed as in the previously described NFT systems.

The multi-channel NFT system should be supported by a wooden or steel frame at waist height to facilitate working with the crop and conveniently positioning the plumbing and solution reservoir.

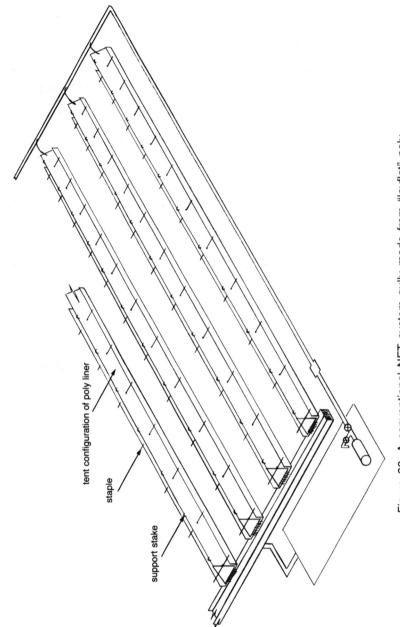

tent configuration of poly liner

staple

support stake

Figure 22. A conventional NFT system gully made from "layflat" poly-ethylene. The gully is held in a tent configuration by support stakes and by stapling between plants.

36

Figure 23. A multi-channel NFT system formed by use of corrugated metal roofing. Irrigation inlet line is in foreground. Channels are covered with a 20-mil-thick vinyl to support plants and keep light out of trays. *Courtesy of Garden Patch Produce, Sarasota, Florida.*

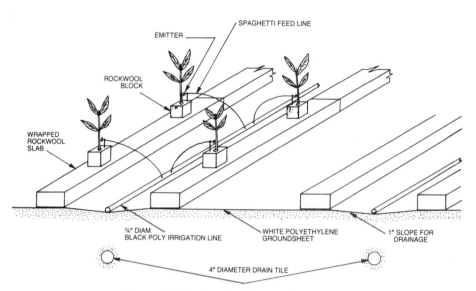

EMITTER

SPAGHETTI FEED LINE

ROCKWOOL
BLOCK

WRAPPED
ROCKWOOL
SLAB

¾" DIAM.
BLACK POLY IRRIGATION LINE

WHITE POLYETHYLENE
GROUNDSHEET

1" SLOPE FOR
DRAINAGE

4" DIAMETER DRAIN TILE

Figure 24. Rockwool culture system.

Figure 25. Rockwool culture with rockwool blocks growing
cucumbers set on slabs. One trickle line feeds each plant.
Courtesy of Environmental Farms, Dundee, Florida.

Rockwool Culture

One of the better methods of growing tomatoes, cucumbers, peppers, melons, and other vine crops is rockwool culture. Its use in commercial greenhouses has increased rapidly over the past decade from several acres to over 5,000 acres (2,000 hectares).

Rockwool is produced as an inert fibrous material by heating a mixture of volcanic rock, limestone, and coke to 2,000° Celsius. It is extruded as fine threads which are pressed into loosely woven sheets. With about 95 percent pore spaces, it has high water retention yet drains well while maintaining its structural integrity.

The pH of rockwool is between 7.0 and 8.5. The pH may be reduced to 6.0–6.5 by soaking the rockwool with an acidic nutrient solution for 24 hours before planting.

Most large commercial rockwool culture operations are designed with an open, non-recirculating hydroponic system (fig. 24). However, on the smaller scale of home gardening, rockwool culture can be set up as a recirculating, or closed, system.

To do this, the rockwool slabs are placed on a vinyl- or polyethylene-lined wooden trough similar to the NFT system. Rockwool slabs come in 36-inch (90 cm) lengths by 6-inch (15 cm) or 8-inch (20 cm) widths. The narrower slabs are used for growing tomatoes and peppers, whereas the wider ones are more suitable for cucumbers and melons.

Wooden supporting troughs constructed of 1-inch by 10-inch bottoms and 1-inch by 2-inch sides are lined with a 6-mil-thick black polyethylene sheet. A two percent slope back to a catchment pipe will conduct the nutrient solution back to a solution reservoir.

The solution is pumped through a 1-inch (2.5 cm) diameter header pipe attached to ½-inch diameter black polyethylene irrigation laterals. One lateral runs the length of the beds between each pair of rows. Then, drip emitters are pressed into the laterals and spaghetti lines lead from the emitters to the base of each plant positioned in the rockwool slabs (fig. 25).

Pressure compensating emitters of two liters per hour volume output are attached directly to the laterals to regulate an even flow of solution. It is best to attach the emitters to the laterals rather than to the ends of the spaghetti lines in order to prevent plugging caused by precipitation of nutrient salts.

Figure 26. Small rockwool propagation cubes (1-inch cube) growing cucumber seedlings (4–5 days old).

Figure 27. The author transplanting cucumber seedlings, started in rockwool cubes, to rockwool blocks.

Sow seeds into small rockwool plugs or directly into 3-inch by 3-inch by 2.5-inch (7.5 by 7.5 by 6.5 cm) blocks (figs. 26–28). It is important to soak these plugs and blocks to saturation (run-off) with nutrient solution prior to sowing the seeds, as that will lower their high pH. For the first seven days from seeding, use a half-strength nutrient solution.

Place the growing blocks in clean plastic flats having drainage holes.

You may sterilize the flats with a 10 percent chlorine bleach solution.

Water the propagation blocks with half strength nutrient solution several times a day. Each time, water to run-off. Never allow the blocks to dry between watering.

It is better to grow the seedlings under supplementary artificial lighting using cool-white, fluorescent light. This will produce healthy, stalky plants. Cucumber seedlings having three to four true leaves are ready to transplant onto the slabs (fig. 29).

Cut three small holes in the top of each slab and insert a spaghetti line in each.

Make up the nutrient solution in the tank using the young plant (7–30 days) formulation from Tables 3 and 4. Pump the solution into the slabs until they are full, allowing them to soak 24 hours. This will adjust the pH and uniformly moisten the slabs.

After soaking, cut drainage holes on the slab sides at the bottom edge. Cut on an angle, about 2 inches (5 cm) in length. Three slits are cut on the inside face (side facing irrigation line), spaced equally along each slab but not directly under the plants.

Transplant two plants per slab at 20-inch (50 cm) centers. Make a 4-inch (10 cm) cross-cut in the top poly liner of the slab where each plant is to be located. After setting the transplant in its position, secure the block to the slab with a stake that also holds the spaghetti lines in place on top of the block (fig. 25). At the time of transplanting, place the lower end of the support string between the rockwool block and the slab to secure it (fig. 30). Plastic stakes with a hook- or wedge-opening end for attaching the spaghetti line are available from greenhouse suppliers. The feeder line should remain in this position for four to five days until the plant roots grow into the slab below. Then the spaghetti lines, with the stakes, are moved onto the slab close to the base of the transplant blocks (fig. 31). Pull back the poly cover of the slab

Figure 28. Cucumber growing in 3" by 3" by 2.5-inch rockwool blocks. With roots penetrating the bottom of the block, the plant is ready to transplant onto the rockwool slabs. By growing the seedlings on mesh trays, the roots are well air-pruned, keeping them in the blocks.

Figure 29. Cucumber seedling with four true leaves ready for transplanting onto the rockwool slab. Note the air-pruning of the roots at the bottom of the block.

Figure 31. Trickle irrigation line set at the edge of the growing block on the slab. Note the support twine wound around the cucumber stem. *Courtesy of Environmental Farms, Dundee, Florida.*

Figure 30. Place the end of the support string between the rockwool block and slab when transplanting. *Courtesy of Environmental Farms, Dundee, Florida.*

43

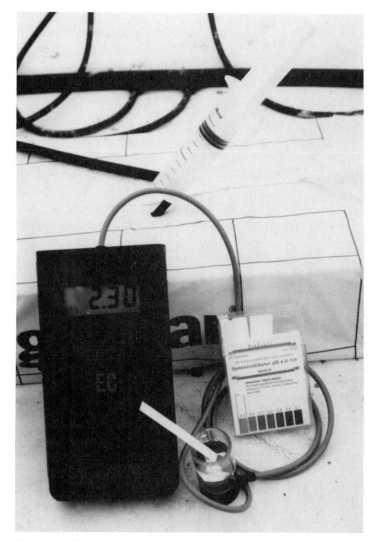

Figure 32. Sampling of rockwool slab with syringe to test pH and EC (electrical conductivity) of the slab solution.

slightly, at the block base, so that the solution will drip onto the rockwool of the slab and not run off the cover.

Frequent irrigation is necessary immediately after transplanting—at least every hour during daylight and several times at night. Once the plant roots have penetrated the slabs, the irrigation frequency can be reduced to 8–10 times daily depending upon the plant stage of growth and environmental conditions. Each irrigation cycle must be three to four minutes to allow a 15–20 percent runoff from the slabs.

A 24-hour time-clock having five-minute intervals is needed to start each irrigation cycle. Alternatively, use two time-clocks: one, a 24-hour with one-hour intervals and another, a one-hour clock with 60-minute intervals wired in series, can operate the pump (the first clock controls the beginning of each cyle; the second, its duration).

Both the pH and the electrical conductivity (EC)—see Chapter 4—of the rockwool slabs are monitored several times a week. The pH should be maintained between 5.8 and 6.4, while the EC should remain between 2.2 and 3.5. The easiest method of testing is to extract several solution samples in the middle of the slab between the plants using a small pointed syringe (fig. 32).

The solution pH is tested with indicator paper. The EC must be tested with a conductivity meter as described in Chapter 4.

The nutrient solution pH is adjusted appropriately with an acid or base as described in Chapter 4. If the EC drops more than 15–20 percent, the same percentage each of parts A and B of the macroelement formulation (Table 3) must be added.

Using the stock solutions outlined in Chapter 4, if the EC of a 100 liter nutrient tank fell by 20 percent over the period of one week, 20 percent of the normal nutrient make-up should be added (20 percent of 1 liter of stock solutions A and B is 200 ml of each). If the EC fluctuates greatly from one week to the next, the nutrient solution will have to be changed. This would normally be at least once a month. You do not need to add any *micro*nutrients when adjusting the EC since they may build-up to toxic levels if added.

Rockwool slabs may be used for several crops provided that they are sterilized between crops. Six to eight slabs can be sterilized in the oven of a stove if the polyethylene wrapping is removed. Heat the slabs to 200° F. for at least one-half hour. Be

Figure 33. Sawdust bag system, growing tomatoes.

sure to wring out excess moisture from the slabs before heating them in the stove.

The growing blocks and propagation cubes cannot be re-used as they become full of roots, fertilizer salts, and algae.

Rockwool slabs are sold as bundles of 12. Growing blocks are sold in cases of 384 for the smaller 3-inch blocks, and 216 pieces for the 4-inch blocks. Propagation cubes come as 30 trays of 98 cubes each (2,940 cubes/case).

These rockwool products may be purchased from greenhouse suppliers or from a distributor (see Appendix). The rockwool slabs cost approximately US $2.50 each, while the growing blocks cost about US $70 a case, and propagation cubes are close to US $100 a case. They are somewhat expensive for growing lettuce and leafy vegetables but are reasonable for the growing of vine crops.

Sawdust Culture

Sawdust culture was once one of the most commonly used commercial soilless systems in forested areas such as the Pacific Northwest of the United States and the west coast of Canada. At present, sawdust is not as readily available and is more costly since it is used in other lumber by-products. However, there are still a number of commercial greenhouse operations growing vegetables in sawdust culture.

For the home gardener, sawdust is an alternative medium to rockwool. Sawdust from Douglas fir and western hemlock give best results. Cedar sawdust is not suitable due to the presence of toxic resins. Before using any sawdust, wash it thoroughly with raw water to remove any residual salt that may have become deposited in it from logs being stored in ocean inlets.

A sawdust culture system can be set up similarly to the rock-wool system. The easiest method is to use common, clear plastic kitchen garbage bags to hold the sawdust (fig. 33). Cut drainage holes in the bottom of the bags and place them on a polyethylene-lined trough or bed somewhat wider than that used for rockwool culture. Such a bed constructed of ¾-inch thick plywood should be about 12 inches (30 cm) wide to allow drainage water to pass along the sides of the bags and return to the solution reservoir via a catchment trench. The remainder of the system is set up the same as for the rockwool system with irrigation lines to each bag (fig. 33).

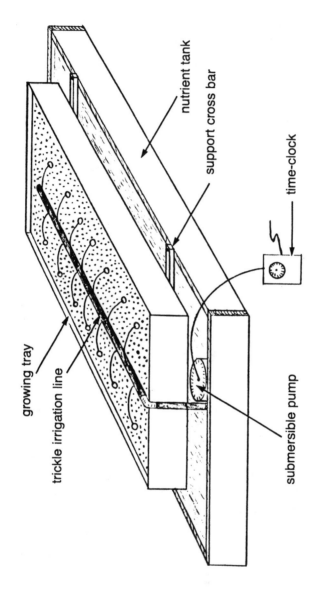

Figure 34. A simple, small-scale, trickle sawdust culture system.

One or two plants can be grown in each bag. At least one spaghetti line should be placed near the base of each plant. If two plants are grown per bag, train the plants in a "V" direction upwards along support strings to allow more light into the crop.

Lateral movement of the nutrient solution on the sawdust surface is improved by covering it with one-inch (2.5 cm) of sand after transplanting.

Seedlings should be grown in either peat pellets or in rockwool blocks as for rockwool culture. The pH and electrical conductivity (EC) of the solution must be monitored and adjusted as described for the rockwool culture.

Smaller indoor units may be constructed with a tray placed on top of a nutrient tank as shown in figure 34. Plants are fed by a trickle irrigation system operated by a pump on a time-clock.

Peat, Perlite, Vermiculite Cultures

These media are generally used as a mixture. Vegetables are not usually grown commercially with these media except in the propagation of seedlings. Their principal use is in the production of potted flowering and ornamental houseplants.

The home grower, however, may use these media for vegetable growing in a manner similar to that of sawdust. Sand is often included with peat and perlite or vermiculite mixes. Some common mixtures are:

1. peat:perlite: sand   2:2:1— for potted plants
2. peat:perlite   1:1 — propagation of cuttings
3. peat:vermiculite   1:1 — propagation of cuttings
4. peat:vermiculite   2:1 — potted plants and
   or perlite   vegetables

A suitable medium mixture for growing vegetables in plastic bags, as outlined in sawdust culture, would be: 70 percent peat and 30 percent vermiculite. Mix the medium thoroughly with a clean shovel on a sterilized concrete floor or a piece of 6-mil-thick polyethylene. Sterilize the floor with a 10 percent chlorine bleach solution. While mixing, add water slowly to moisten the peat. The addition of two ounces (56 g) of wetting agent in 10 gallons (38 l) of water will facilitate wetting the peat in one cubic yard (0.76 cu m) of mix.

Moisten the medium until you can squeeze a handful and it

Figure 35. Small indoor unit of two-chambered tank. Nutrient solution is pumped to vermiculite-filled upper tray by aquarium pump.

remains in a ball that breaks apart slowly but no water runs from it. This is about the right moisture level for placing it into the plastic garbage bags. If you add too much water, it will pack, reducing its porosity.

Peat is very acid with a pH of 4.0 to 5.0 depending upon its source. This low pH should be corrected before planting. Raise the pH by adding 11 pounds (5 kg) of dolomite limestone per cubic yard (0.76 cu m) during mixing.

Smaller indoor units can use vermiculite alone as a growing medium. While perlite is also suitable, it is so light in weight that it floats, sometimes plugging irrigation lines. Do not attempt to sterilize these media between crops; simply replace them.

A number of indoor units are shown in figures 35–37. A deeper tank, holding the growing medium, sits on top of a shallower tank with a slightly larger base which serves as the nutrient solution reservoir. The bottom of the upper tank is perforated to allow drainage back to the solution tank.

Such two-chambered hydroponic units are sold by a number of manufacturers.

An aquarium pump is used to disperse air into a tube submerged in the nutrient solution. The nutrient solution flows into the tube through a hole, or past the walls of a slightly larger diameter tube in which the air pump tube is held by a pin (fig. 38). This mixture of air and nutrient solution flows up the tube to the top of the growing medium. The tube is perforated along the top to allow the solution to bleed from the tube along its length onto the surface of the medium. The solution percolates through the root zone, down through the medium, and back into the solution reservoir via the perforated bottom of the medium-holding tank.

There is an even simpler and less expensive method of growing herbs and lettuce. Use a plastic flat, without drainage holes, and a filler tray having 24 or 36 compartments such as those used for growing bedding plants (fig. 39). These flats are 10½ by 21 inches in size.

Remove one of the compartments at one corner and place a one-gallon plastic bottle in that location (fig. 39). This nutrient bottle must have a large plastic cap through which a small hole (about ¼-inch diameter) is drilled and to which a split cork ring is glued (fig. 40). The cork ring should be about 2½–3 inches in diameter so the bottle will be stable when turned upside down.

Figure 36. Small indoor unit.

Figure 37. Small indoor unit.

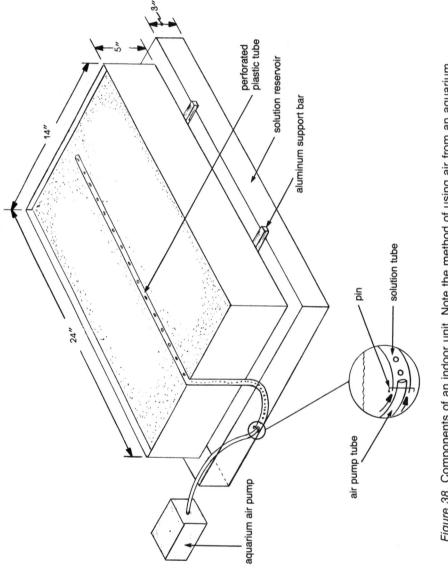

5"

3"

14"

24"

perforated
plastic tube

solution reservoir

aluminum support bar

pin

solution tube

air pump tube

aquarium air pump

Figure 38. Components of an indoor unit. Note the method of using air from an aquarium pump to force the nutrient solution up the tube to the growing tray.

Figure 39. Plastic flat with nutrient bottle reservoir to grow herbs and lettuce.

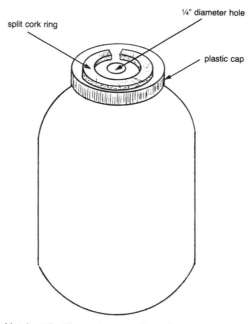

Figure 40. Nutrient bottle and cap with split cork ring to regulate solution flow into the growing tray.

The bottle is filled with nutrient solution and inverted into the flat. The hole in the cap allows the solution to flow out of the bottle until the air supply is cut off as the level of solution in the tray reaches the hole.

As the plants use up the solution, the level falls, allowing more air to enter the bottle and the solution to leave it.

The seed should germinate before you place the nutrient bottle in the tray. First, fill the compartments of the tray with coarse vermiculite. Sow the seeds directly into the vermiculite and cover them with a finer vermiculite crushed by hand. Moisten the seeds and medium with raw water, then cover the tray with black polyethylene sheeting for several days until germination occurs. Once the seeds germinate, remove the plastic immediately, move the tray to full light, and then place the solution bottle in it.

This type of starter tray is ideal for growing small plants such as herbs, bedding plants for later transplanting, and for leaf lettuce. You must harvest the lettuce after 14–21 days when it reaches 3–4 inches (8–10 cm) in height, before overcrowding causes it to stretch. You can easily cut it off at the surface of the medium with scissors. This will be some of the most tender lettuce you have ever eaten!

Most of these indoor units are about 1 by 2 feet (30 by 60 cm) in dimension, having two square feet of growing area.

Larger units, 18 inches (45 cm) wide by up to 6–8 feet (1.8–2.4 m) in length, can be constructed in a similar manner. This larger system can be used in a backyard greenhouse to grow both vine crops and leafy vegetables.

A nutrient reservoir of 2 by 6 feet (60 cm by 1.8 m) can support a growing tray of slightly smaller dimensions.

The nutrient reservoir, about 3–4 inches (7.5–10 cm) deep, may be constructed of wood, lined with vinyl or polyethylene. Wood or aluminum cross bars at 18-inch (46 cm) centers not only prevent the tank from bowing outward but also support the upper growing tray (fig. 41).

The upper tray could be constructed of wooden sides about 5–6 inches (12–15 cm) deep with a double fiberglass screen bottom. Or you may use a plastic or fiberglass tray or even a flower box, available from your nearby garden or hydroponics supply center. Drill ¼-inch diameter holes at 3- by 3-inch spacing in the bottom for drainage.

Four or five inches (10-12 cm) of vermiculite is placed in the growing tray.

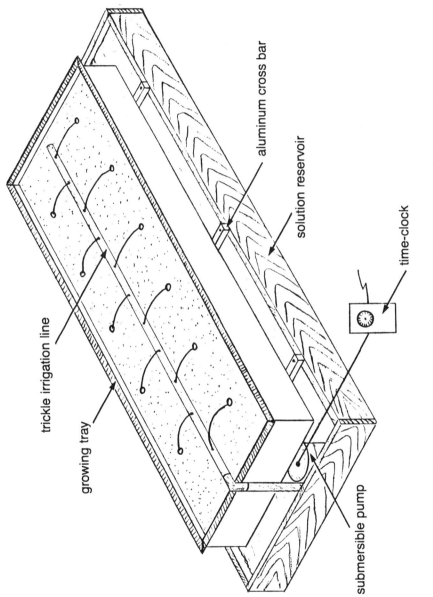

aluminum cross bar

solution reservoir

time-clock

trickle irrigation line

growing tray

submersible pump

Figure 41. Larger indoor unit using a submersible pump in the reservoir under the growing tray.

57

Instead of using an aquarium pump, put a submersible pump, operated by a time-clock, in the solution tank. Attach a ½-inch diameter black polyethylene hose from the pump, extending over the surface of the medium in the top tray. On both sides of this hose insert emitters with spaghetti lines every six inches (15 cm). Position the output end of these feeder lines at the base of the plants.

Vertical Sack Culture

Vertical sack, or column, culture is a good method for hydroponically growing foliage house plants, annuals, flowering plants, strawberries, lettuce, spinach, and herbs.

To grow fruiting vegetables and strawberries you must have full sunlight. The more sunlight you have, the better will be your production. Backyard greenhouses or covered patios having a southern exposure are ideal for growing hydroponically.

Black or opaque white, 6-mil-thick polyethylene tubes approximately 2½ inches (6 cm) in diameter by 4 feet (1.2 m) in length, are filled with a mixture of peat and vermiculite and suspended vertically (fig. 42). The medium should be prepared with dolomite lime as explained under "Peat, Perlite, Vermiculite Cultures," above. Seedlings are inserted through the polyethylene at appropriate intervals.

The nutrient solution percolates from a reservoir on top through a wick incorporated in the medium the length of the sack. A collecting cup at the bottom prevents loss of nutrient solution through drainage.

An alternative to polyethylene tubes, which can easily tear, are 2½-inch diameter PVC pipes. Holes are drilled spirally around the pipe at the appropriate spacing for the crop grown. For example, such holes would be spaced 7 inches (18 cm) apart for lettuce.

If these holes are drilled in a spiral at an angle of 45 degrees from vertical and made slightly smaller than the correct outside diameter of a ¾-inch PVC pipe. Small, 1½-inch-long pieces of ¾-inch pipe can be glued into the holes. These short pipes will provide support for the plants (fig. 43).

The solution can be recirculated by setting the columns in vinyl-lined wood, or metal, gullies containing about one inch (2.5 cm) of coarse sand or pea gravel. A catchment trench conveys the recovered solution to a reservoir for reuse. Then it is pumped back, via a supply line and spaghetti feed lines, to the columns.

Figure 42. Sack culture for growing ornamentals and leafy vegetables vertically.

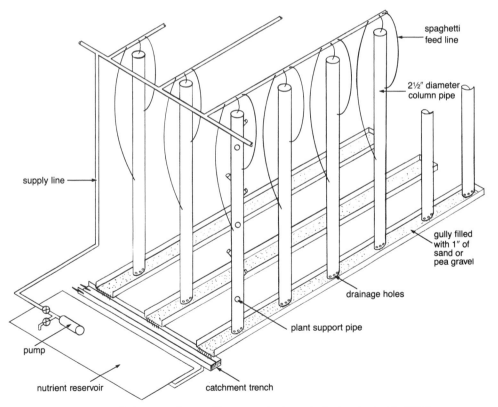

Figure 43. Column culture with support pipes in holes to hold plants.

The columns may be filled with vermiculite with the bottom ends having drainage holes drilled into the end cap and sides.

There is no advantage in growing vine crops in a vertical position. They are normally trained up string supports, creating their own vertical canopy.

Sand Culture

Sand culture is a hydroponic method widely used commercially in desert regions of the world. The Environmental Research Laboratory, University of Arizona, has been instrumental in developing sand culture in such areas. It is not a popular method for the home gardener due to the weight of the sand and the difficulty in sterilizing it between crops.

Sand, nonetheless, is a good medium for hydroponic backyard greenhouses, using either beds or simple plastic pots. A coarse, igneous (quartz-calcite), riverwash sand is best. A mortar sand, with its high percentage of fines (clay, silt) causes puddling which leads to oxygen deficit. Puddling is evident if water comes to the surface upon vibration of the sand. The sand should be washed free of silt and clay. It should be relatively free of particles over 1/16-inch (2 mm) in diameter and under 1/40-inch (0.6 mm).

If you wish to use sand culture, you can start by constructing above-ground beds with wooden sides. These beds should be about 2 feet (60 cm) wide by the greenhouse length. Use 1- by 8-inch rough cedar for the sides. Stake the sides with steel rebar (reinforcing rod) every two to three feet (60–90 cm) to prevent their collapsing from the weight of the sand.

The bottom should be shaped like a shallow "V," achieved by digging the soil so that the bottom slopes from the sides toward the center (fig. 44). The depth of the "V" should be approximately 4 inches (10 cm) at the center. The bed is lined with 20-mil vinyl or 6-mil black polyethylene.

For drainage, lay a 2½-inch diameter PVC pipe along the bottom of the "V" that was formed. On the bottom of the pipe, drill holes 12 inches apart along the pipe's length—or you can make saw cuts one-third of the way through the pipe, at the same intervals of spacing. This drainage pipe connects to a common header from all beds and conducts the waste solution away from the growing area.

Sand culture utilizes an open system, without recycling the nutrient solution.

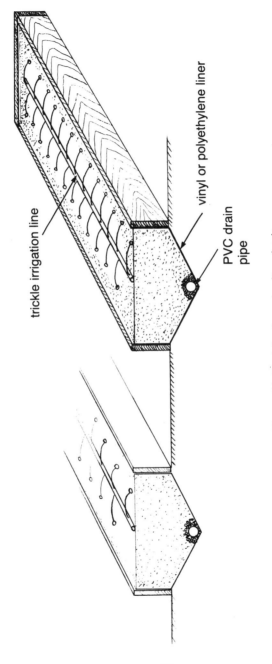

trickle irrigation line

vinyl or polyethylene liner

PVC drain pipe

Figure 44. Sketch of sand culture beds.

61

The nutrient solution is pumped from a tank along a header to which is connected a trickle irrigation system carrying the solution to each plant. During each irrigation, 10–15 percent of the solution applied is drained from the growing beds as waste to avoid salt build-up in the sand. Each drip emitter of the trickle system should apply one-half gallon (about two liters) of solution per hour.

A time-clock operates the pump for 3–4-minute cycles four or five times per day, depending on the stage of plant growth and environmental conditions. (More frequent cycles are required for mature plants under summer conditions.)

As mentioned above, a major disadvantage in the use of sand by a home gardener is the difficulty of sterilizing it between crops. Sand is usually steam sterilized. A 10-percent chlorine bleach solution, as used in other kinds of growing media, cannot be used in sand, as it is difficult to remove all the chlorine bleach from the sand after sterilizing.

Sand may be used for smaller indoor units where it can be sterilized by heating to 200° F. for 30 minutes in the oven of a kitchen stove.

A simple indoor unit can be constructed, using several small trays. Such a tray, one by two feet, can be supported above a nutrient reservoir by several aluminum cross members (fig. 45). (The growing tray could even be a rigid plastic tote bin.)

The lower reservoir can be of wood, lined with polyethylene or vinyl. Irrigation is accomplished by a trickle feed system operated by a pump and a time-clock. The growing tray must be perforated on the bottom as described above to allow drainage back to the reservoir. The nutrient solution in this case, unlike that of the larger beds, is recirculated.

Aggregate Culture

Most of the earliest methods of hydroponics used some form of aggregate (gravel) as a medium. Gravel culture was especially useful on nonarable islands having an abundance of volcanic rock. Because of the low water retention and high porosity of gravel media, a subirrigation system, flooding and draining on a recirculating basis, is used.

Igneous (volcanic origin) rather than calcareous (sedimentary) rocks must be used to avoid pH shifts associated with the release of carbonates from limestones.

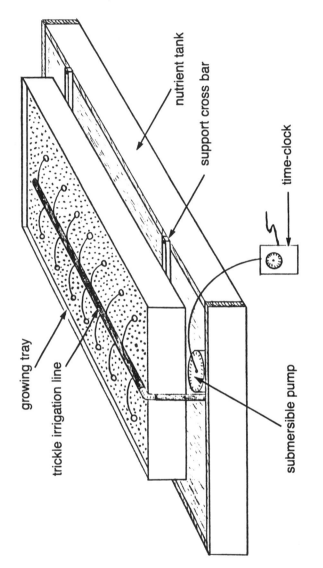

Figure 45. A simple small-scale trickle sand culture system.

growing tray

trickle irrigation line

nutrient tank

support cross bar

time-clock

submersible pump

63

The best gravel is crushed granite of irregular shape, free of fine particles less than 1/16-inch (1.6 mm) in diameter and coarse particles greater than 3/4-inch (1.9 cm) in diameter. The majority of particles should be 3/8–1/2-inch (1–1.3 cm) in diameter.

An alternative to igneous gravel is fired-clay, light-weight aggregate that is a rusty brown in color. This is manufactured by heating clay and expanding it. It is irregular in shape and somewhat porous, giving it higher water retention properties than natural gravel. Its light weight is an advantage to the home grower, but it does break down over a number of years, requiring eventual replacement. "Pea" gravel between 1/8-inch and 3/8-inch (3 mm and 9.5 mm) in diameter can be substituted for the larger aggregate, provided a trickle feeding system is used instead of subirrigation.

All aggregate can be easily sterilized between crops with a 10 percent chlorine bleach solution followed by rinsing with raw water. This is a great advantage for the home gardener.

In a subirrigation system the nutrient solution is pumped from a central tank into the beds, flooding them within an inch of the surface. The solution then drains back as the pump is turned off. Such a closed or recirculating system uses the same nutrient solution repeatedly for each cycle for a period of from 3–6 weeks before the solution is replaced.

The frequency and length of time of irrigation cycles must be such as to provide adequate water, nutrients, and oxygen to plant roots. This frequency and length of each irrigation cycle is a function of the characteristics of the aggregate, stage of plant growth, and environmental conditions. Maximum frequency and length of irrigations would be for mature crops under hot summer conditions. This might be as often as every hour during daylight at such times.

As the nutrient solution fills the void spaces of the aggregate, it pushes out air relatively low in oxygen and high in carbon dioxide. Then, as the solution drains back to the reservoir, it pulls in new air higher in oxygen. Too-frequent irrigation cycles may be damaging, as the void spaces become saturated rather than filled with moist air. Generally, a period of 10–15 minutes for filling and draining is optimum.

Complete drainage is imperative so that only a film of solution remains on the aggregate in contact with plant roots. Rapid fill and drainage is achieved by use of a perforated fill/drain pipe along the bottom of the bed. If the beds are filled only to within one inch of the aggregate surface, the dry surface will discourage algae growth.

In constructing a subirrigation system you must keep in mind that the nutrient tank must be large enough to contain at least 1.3 times the total void space in the growing beds. This may be calculated by taking a known volume of gravel (a cubic foot = 28 liters) in a five-gallon bucket (20 liters) and filling it with water unit it reaches the surface. You would need $28/20$ or 1.4 bucketfuls for a volume of one cubic foot of gravel. The volume of water used is equal to the total void spaces. You then calculate the total void space volume by multiplying the total aggregate volume (cubic feet) in the bed(s) by the volume of water used to fill the void spaces of the one-cubic-foot sample of medium. Add 30 percent as a safety factor.

The nutrient reservoir will require an automatic float assembly to replace spent nutrient solution. Install a gate valve on the water line going to the float valve so that you can regulate the fill rate to be fairly slow. Otherwise, during each irrigation, when the solu-tion is pumped into the beds, the "make-up" volume supplied to the reservoir (since the level drops below the set float level for refilling) may exceed the actual volume needed and the tank will overflow when the beds are drained.

For use in a backyard greenhouse, you may design the subirriga-tion beds as follows. They should be about 24 inches (60 cm) wide with a depth of 12 inches (30 cm), and a bottom with a slight "V" configuration (for drainage) as was described for sand culture beds (fig. 44).

The beds are lined with a 20-mil vinyl and a $2^{1}/_{2}$ inch (6 cm) diameter fill/drain PVC pipe placed at the bottom. Solution enters and drains from the beds via small $1/_{4}$–$3/_{8}$-inch (0.6–1 cm) holes or $1/_{8}$-inch (0.3 cm) thick saw cuts on the bottom one-third of the pipe. These holes, or saw cuts, are made every foot along the pipe's length.

The drain pipe should have a 45-degree elbow at the far end and project above the gravel surface to allow cleaning of roots from the pipe in the future with a drain cleaner (roto-rooter).

If the system contains more than one bed, the fill/drain pipes must themselves be connected to a larger diameter (3-inch) header pipe which, in turn, is connected to a sump pump.

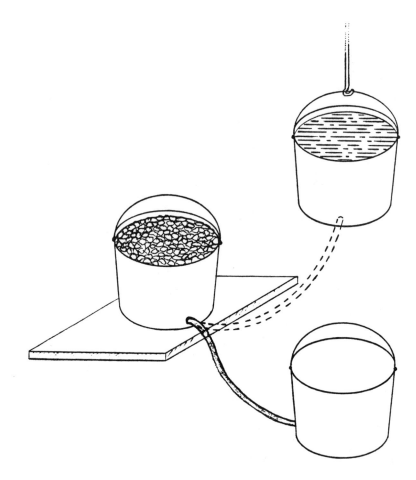

Figure 46. Bucket system of gravel culture.

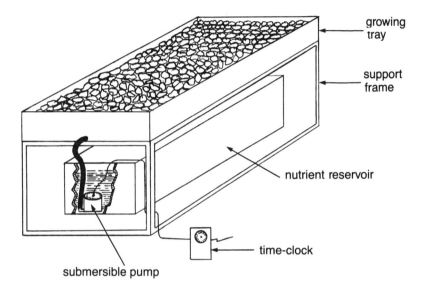

growing tray

support frame

nutrient reservoir

time-clock

submersible pump

Figure 47. A simple, small-scale subirrigation gravel bed with auto-matic pumping.

One of the earliest, simple gravel culture indoor units was the bucket system (fig. 46). Plants are grown in a small bucket of gravel set on a bench. A second bucket containing the nutrient solution, is connected to the other by a hose. The second bucket, normally on the floor, is raised above the level of the first to make the solution flow to the plants. Once the growing bucket fills up, the reservoir bucket is lowered for drainage.

This same principle can be expanded to a series of buckets, each attached to a larger growing bed, as long as the total volume of solution in all buckets is at least equivalent to the total void space of the growing medium in the bed.

Of course, such a laborious and time-consuming method is not popular today. We can, however, use the same principles, but simply add a pump operated by a time-clock to the reservoir. The pump is connected to the growing tray with plastic piping so that when it is inactive the solution runs back to the reservoir through the pump (fig. 47).

Another simple home unit is one using a trickle feeding system with "pea" or fired-clay gravel medium. A reservoir under a growing bed stores the solution which is pumped via "spaghetti" feeder lines over the gravel surface to the base of each plant (fig. 48). Excess water drains back to the reservoir underneath via the perforated tray end, or bottom. Once again, the irrigation cycles are operated by a time-clock.

The reservoir may be constructed of wood, lined with vinyl, with several aluminum tube cross members to support the growing tray above. A restaurant plastic tote bin may be used for the plant tray. Simply drill drainage holes in the bottom of the tote bin before filling it with the gravel.

The trickle irrigation design of aggregate culture is most suitable to backyard greenhouse operators (fig. 49). For backyard greenhouses up to 20 feet (6 m) in length, the beds may be designed somewhat shallower and without the fill-drain pipe required by subirrigation systems. You may construct raised beds of 2-inch by 4-inch wood framing and 5/8–3/4-inch-thick plywood. The beds should be 24 inches (60 cm) wide and lined with 20-mil vinyl (fig. 50).

After painting the beds, staple the vinyl at the top edges of the beds, and cover those edges and top of the bed sides with a strip of 2-inch (5-cm) wide ducting tape (figs. 50, 51). Add a drain by drilling a 2-inch diameter hole in the center of the bottom within

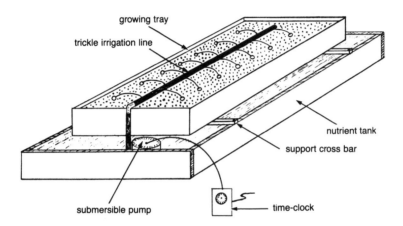

Figure 48. A simple, small-scale trickle gravel bed with automatic pumping.

Figure 49. Pea gravel culture with trickle irrigation to each plant.

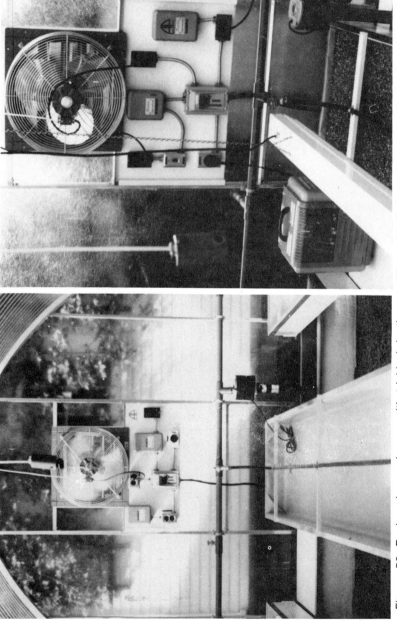

Figure 50. Backyard greenhouse with trickle irrigation gravel culture system. Two-foot-wide beds are constructed of plywood, lined with vinyl. *Courtesy of Resh Greenhouses Ltd., Vancouver, B.C.*

Figure 51. Hydroponic system of a backyard greenhouse (10½- by 12 feet). Note the location of the control panel and sump pump at the rear, and the nutrient tank set perpendicularly, under the lower ends of the beds. The irrigation system consists of a header line connected to laterals running along each bed.

one inch of the end of the bed. Fit a 3-inch (7.5 cm) long piece of PVC pipe tightly into the hole, after cutting through the vinyl. A thin-wall, 2-inch diameter PVC pipe three inches long can be cut longitudinally at the end and pressed together to, in effect, reduce its diameter slightly so that it will fit into the drainage hole. Cut the vinyl above the drain hole in a star configuration and apply some vinyl glue on the cut ends before pushing the drain pipe into the hole. The glue will seal the vinyl around the outside of the drain pipe.

The beds may be supported by concrete blocks. Be sure to slope the beds (about 2 inches for each 10 feet [3 m] of length) towards a nutrient reservoir placed perpendicular to the drain ends of the beds (fig. 50). The nutrient reservoir may be constructed of wood, lined with 20-mil vinyl. For a greenhouse having three beds of 10–12 feet in length, a minimum 70-gallon tank is needed.

A sealed, submersible pump or a sump pump with a plastic impeller will resist the highly corrosive nutrient solution (fig. 50).

A plastic header pipe positioned at the back of the greenhouse has one ½-inch diameter black polyethylene lateral running the length of each bed (figs. 50, 51).

Aluminum tube cross members attached to the bed edges placed every three feet (one meter) support both the bed and the trickle irrigation line (fig. 50). Simply screw U-clamps around the feed line to secure it to the cross supports.

Spaghetti lines and emitters should be installed every six inches (15 cm) on both sides of each lateral so that each plant receives a line at its base (fig. 52).

Many crops can be grown successfully with this medium (figs. 53–55).

Roots build up in the gravel with each successive crop until a large mat forms on the bottom of the bed. You can prevent future drainage problems by removing these roots annually. Simply turn over the gravel with your hands or a shovel—carefully so as not to tear the vinyl liner. Rinse the accumulated sand or silt with water.

The gravel medium is easily sterilized with a 10 percent chlorine bleach solution.

Figure 52. Spaghetti lines are placed at the base of each plant. Note the tomato seedlings growing in peat pellets in the plastic flat.

Figure 53. Lettuce, chard, herbs, and tomatoes growing in light-weight, fired-clay rock aggregate.

Figure 54. Parsley, chard, and tomatoes growing in fired-clay rock aggregate.

Figure 55. Mature crop of tomatoes growing in fired-clay rock.

Summary

There are many different systems of hydroponics suitable for you as a home gardener. Your choice depends on what plants you wish to grow, your budget, availability of materials, the system's size, and the degree of automation you desire.

Some systems may be available complete and ready-to-use from hydroponic suppliers (see Appendix).

Whatever the system you may decide on, remember that the composition of your nutrient solution as well as its pH and EC will greatly influence your success, as will the amount of natural sunlight available to the plants.

Fruiting crops, such as tomatoes, cucumbers, and peppers, are sun-loving, whereas leafy vegetables are somewhat less demanding of light but not really shade tolerant like tropical foliage plants.

An added benefit of hydroponics is that you may use the nutrient solution on most house plants as well as those in your garden. Since houseplants are grown in a soilless mixture of peat, perlite, or vermiculite, they need to obtain all their nutrients from a prepared "plant food." What better food for them than your nutrient solution, which contains all the essential nutritional elements.

CHAPTER 2

Plant Nutrition and Hydroponic Growing Beds

This chapter discusses the minerals essential for plants as well as their function in the plants, symptoms of mineral deficiencies, control of pH (acid-alkaline) and EC (electrical conductivity) in regulating plant nutrition.

The function and composition of the nutrient solution is described, with a number of nutrient formulations for growing cucumbers, tomatoes, peppers, lettuce, and leafy vegetables.

Step-by-step instructions for preparing the nutrient solution and its pH adjustment are presented.

We learn about various kinds of soilless growing media and how to sterilize them between crops.

Essential Elements and Their Function

Plants require 16 essential elements to grow and reproduce. These elements include oxygen, carbon, and hydrogen, the basic building blocks for all organic compounds (sugars, starches, proteins, lipids, and nucleic acids).

Oxygen comes from three sources: water, gaseous oxygen (O_2), and carbon dioxide (CO_2) in the atmosphere. Carbon comes from the carbon dioxide in the air. Hydrogen is obtained from water. These three elements (C, H, O) make up over 95 percent of the plant's dry weight. The fresh weight of a plant is typically 80 percent or more of water.

The remaining 13 essential elements are minerals—naturally occurring inorganic substances in the earth. Minerals become available to plants as ions, dissolved in soil water as discussed in The Life and Growth of Plants. Table 1 lists the main functions of the mineral elements, together with symptoms expected with their deficiency.

Soil vs. Soilless Culture

Plant physiology (function) is similar in either soil or soilless culture. Plants take up water and minerals in the same way, whether they are growing in soil or in any other medium. The essential elements must be available to the plant roots in either the soil, in the one case, or from the nutrient solution in the other.

The advantage of the hydroponic method is that you can regulate the available nutrients in the nutrient solution better than you can in the natural solution that is formed by water in the soil. In soilless culture, you have control over the proportions and quantities of nutrients, whereas in soil culture you don't. You hope that the soil particles release the nutrients in correct proportions to the water in the soil and form a balanced solution of nutrients for use by the plants.

Once nutrients are added to soil, there is no easy method to change or reduce their concentrations. In a hydroponic system, the nutrient solution can be adjusted or changed to suit the particular stage of plant growth or changing environmental conditions.

Optimization of nutrition in a soilless system can more easily be achieved, but remember that it is also easier to damage plants due to a serious error in making up the nutrient solution. For instance, if an element is inadvertently left out of a solution, its absence would soon cause a deficiency in the crop.

If you buy nutrient mixtures commercially, or if you exercise reasonable care in making your own, this should not be a prob-lem.

The pH must be tested every day and the solution adjusted if necessary. In a hydroponic system there is little buffering capac-ity, whereas in soil, nutrients are adsorbed (taken up and held) by the soil particles and released more slowly. This exchange be-tween soil particles and the soil solution stabilizes (buffers) any large nutrient and pH shifts.

An understanding of plant nutrition, pH, and EC (electrical conductivity) will greatly assist you in maintaining your nutrient solution at optimum quality for maximum productivity.

Growing Medium

The medium—the material in which plants grow—must pro-vide water, oxygen, nutrients, and support for plant roots. With hydroponics, any sterile medium having a structure and composi-tion that provides adequate root anchorage and oxygenation will be suitable. Typical media include gravel, sand, peat, vermiculite, perlite, pumice, a mixture of these latter four, sawdust, rockwool, styrofoam beads, fired clay particles, rice hulls, or just water alone. The nutrient solution provides water, nutrients, and some oxygen.

Particle size, shape, and porosity determine the medium's moisture retention capacity. The nutrient solution is retained on the surface of the particles and within the pore spaces. Smaller particles pack closer, resulting in greater surface area and pore space, giving the medium high water retention. Irregular-shaped particles have greater surface area and water retention than smooth, round, particles. Water retention is higher in porous materials. Excessively fine materials must be avoided in order to allow good drainage and oxygenation to roots.

The choice of medium is dependent on availability, cost, quality, cleanliness, and the crop to be grown. For example, while lettuce grows well in water culture, tomatoes, cucumbers, and peppers do not.

Table 1: Role of Elements in Plant Function

Element	Function	Deficiency Symptoms
MACROELEMENTS		
Nitrogen (N)	Synthesis of organic compounds, including amino acids, proteins, coenzymes, nucleic acids and chlorophyll.	General yellowing (chlorosis) especially of older leaves, lower leaves yellow and die, growth is stunted, younger leaves remain green longer as the mobile nitrogen is retranslocated from older leaves to younger ones; first symptoms on older leaves.
Phosphorus (P)	Component of sugar phosphates (energy carrier), nucleic acids, phospholipids and coenzymes.	Stunted growth, dark green in color, purplish leaves and stems. As it is easily redistributed from older to younger tissues, first symptoms occur in mature older leaves.
Potassium (K)	Protein synthesis, acts as a coenzyme (activator) for many enzymes, sugar and starch formation, needed in plant growth.	Like N and P it can be easily retranslocated from mature leaves to younger plant parts; first symptoms on older leaves. Spindly plants, yellowing of older leaves followed by scattered dead areas. Tips and margins of older leaves often die first.
Calcium (Ca)	Component of cell walls, cell growth and division.	As it is immobile (cannot be retranslocated), symptoms first appear in younger leaves, especially the growing tip. Deformed terminal leaves, growing tip dies, root growth is inhibited.
Magnesium (Mg)	Part of chlorophyll, photosynthesis.	Mobile element—first symptoms as interveinal and marginal chlorosis of lower leaves. Dark, dead (necrotic) spots later appear in the chlorotic areas; finally older leaves die, fruit production is reduced.
Sulfur (S)	Present in some amino acids, vitamins.	General yellowing of plant, reduced growth similar to nitrogen deficiency; relatively immobile—first symptoms on younger leaves.

Table 1: Role of Elements in Plant Function *(continued)*

Element	Function	Deficiency Symptoms
MINOR OR TRACE ELEMENTS		
Iron (Fe)	Activator (catalyst) in chlorophyll synthesis, electron transport in photosynthesis and respiration.	Immobile—first symptoms in tip—chlorosis of young leaves. Initially small veins remain green, leaves eventually turn completely pale yellow, no necrosis; stunting of growth, flower abortion.
Manganese (Mn)	Activates enzymes (coenzyme), chlorophyll synthesis.	Immobile—veins of young leaves remain green while interveinal tissue yellows, giving a reticular green pattern on a yellow background. Stunted growth, necrotic spots later develop in chlorotic areas.
Boron (B)	Transport of photosynthates, affects flowering, fruiting.	Immobile—growing point dies, side shoots begin to grow, then die. Leaves thicken, curl inward, deform, and become brittle, stunting.
Zinc (Zn)	Part of certain enzymes, formation of chlorophyll, growth regulators.	Mobile—first symptoms in older leaves, interveinal chlorosis. Leaves coil up, stunting—short internodes, leads to closely spaced upper leaves.
Copper (Cu)	Part of certain enzymes, synthesis of chlorophyll.	Immobile—middle and younger leaves. Margins curl into a tube, terminal leaves small, stunted growth, leaf petioles bend downward.
Molybdenum (Mo)	Present in certain enzymes needed for nitrate reduction	All leaves pale green to yellowish; interveinal mottling, leaf margins curl upward, necrosis develops in chlorotic areas, younger leaves remain green.
Chlorine (Cl)	Stimulation of photosynthesis, needed in root and shoot growth.	Wilting of leaves—become chlorotic and necrotic, bronzing of leaves, stunting of roots.

The medium must not contain any toxic substances (sawdust, for example, often contains sodium chloride—salt—from the sea water in which the logs have been transported).

Calcareous gravel and sand (containing lime or calcium) should be avoided—igneous materials should be used instead. Igneous materials have little affect on the nutrient solution's pH, whereas calcareous substances will buffer the solution's pH close to 7.5— too alkaline.

Sterilization of the Medium

To prevent any carry-over of pests and diseases from one crop to the next, the medium should be sterilized after each crop, or changed completely, depending on what kind of medium it is. As crops are continuously grown in any medium, "soil-borne" pests and diseases may accumulate in the medium, with the chances of an outbreak increasing with each successive crop.

Inert, rigid media, such as gravel and sand, may be sterilized by soaking with a 10 percent chlorine bleach solution for at least half an hour, followed by flushing with clean water.

Other media, such as peat, vermiculite, perlite, sawdust, and rockwool, may either be replaced entirely or sterilized by steaming at 180°F for at least half an hour. Generally, the easiest procedure for the home gardener is to simply replace the media between crops, or every other crop, if he is using one of the easily replaceable media mentioned above.

Growing beds used for water culture systems can simply be scrubbed with a 10 percent chlorine bleach solution.

Nutrient Solution

The nutrient solution in hydroponics, like the in-the-soil solution in traditional gardening, provides the plant roots with water and essential elements. In hydroponics, the essential elements are added to the nutrient solution, using fertilizer salts.

On a commercial scale, the choice of suitable fertilizers may be influenced by cost, availability, and quality. As a home gardener, you can use higher grades of fertilizer salts, if you wish, since cost may not be as important to you, in the quantities you will use, as it is to commercial growers.

Your garden or hydroponic supplier may offer ready-prepared nutrient formulations, if you find the storing of bags of individual fertilizers inconvenient.

Whatever form of fertilizer is used, it must be highly soluble in water. It is better to dissolve all fertilizers in hot water prior to adding them to the water in the hydroponic nutrient solution tank or reservoir.

Water Quality

Water quality is important in hydroponics. Good quality water should be relatively soft, with a maximum sodium chloride content of 50 parts per million (ppm). Plant growth is restricted by high sodium chloride levels. Water hardness is a measure of carbonate ion (HCO_3) content. As hardness increases, so does pH. Certain essential elements such as iron become unavailable at high pH.

Hard waters, containing calcium and magnesium are suitable, provided that the nutrient formulation is adjusted to take into account the presence of these elements, reducing the amount you will add in making up your formula. Levels of calcium and magnesium can be determined by a water analysis—possibly available from your municipal water department or other water supplier, or from an independent testing laboratory.

While many prepared plant foods are available in hydroponic or garden centers, and even in supermarkets, it is cheaper, more versatile and more challenging to make up your own formulations. Most of the compounds needed to supply all the essential elements in your hydroponic fertilizer mix can be purchased from garden centers or directly from fertilizer companies. Some of the micronutrient salts such as boric acid (H_3BO_3) can be obtained from pharmacies. Table 2 outlines the fertilizers required to supply the various nutrients.

Nutrient Formulations

This book is not intended to teach you how to actually calculate nutrient formulas. More detailed coverage of the subject is presented in advanced books such as *Hydroponic Food Production* by this author (Woodbridge Press). A list of reference books is given in the Appendix.

The objective here is to give you a number of formulations suitable to the most popular vegetables such as tomatoes, cucumbers, and leafy crops (lettuce, spinach, herbs, chard, etc.), and a combination of food crops.

Table 2: Fertilizer Salts for Hydroponics

Fertilizer	Chemical Formula	Elements Supplied
A. MACROELEMENTS		
Potassium Nitrate (Saltpeter)	KNO_3	K, N
Calcium Nitrate	$Ca\,(NO_3)_2$	Ca, N
Potassium Sulfate	K_2SO_4	K, S
Monopotassium Phosphate	KH_2PO_4	K, P
Magnesium Sulfate (Epsom salts)	$MgSO_4$	Mg, S
Phosphoric Acid	H_3PO_4	P
B. MICROELEMENTS		
Iron Chelate (Sequestrene 330)	FeEDTA	Fe
Boric Acid	H_3BO_3	B
Sodium Borate (Borax)	$Na_2B_4O_7$	B
Copper Sulfate (Bluestone)	$CuSO_4$	Cu, S
Manganese Sulfate	$MnSO_4$	Mn, S
Manganese Chloride	$MnCl_2$	Mn, Cl
Zinc Sulfate	$ZnSO_4$	Zn, S
Zinc Chloride	$ZnCl_2$	Zn, Cl
Ammonium Molybdate	$(NH_4)_6Mo_7O_{24}$	Mo, N

Levels of various nutrients are expressed as parts per million (ppm) or milligrams per liter (mg/l). Parts per million is based on a specified number of units by weight of the fertilizer salt for each million parts of solution. One ppm is equivalent to one milligram of the fertilizer salt per liter of solution (mg/l).

A number of nutrient formulae are presented in Table 3. These formulae are for the *macroelements*. A standard *microelement* formula may be used with each of the macroelement formulae to complete it. Since very small weights of micronutrients are required, it is better to make up a liquid concentrate stock solution which can then be added to your final nutrient solution. To measure accurately, a balance accurate to 0.01 grams is required.

The table assumes that *no* elements are present in the raw water. If a water analysis reveals significant amounts of calcium or magnesium, the quantities of salts used must be reduced accordingly. For example, if a water analysis reveals 15 ppm of calcium and 20 ppm of magnesium, the amount to be added would be changed from that shown under "cucumbers," for example, using this equation:

$$\text{Ca:} \quad \frac{245 - 15}{245} \text{ X } 100 = 94 \text{ g/100 liters}$$

$$\text{Mg:} \quad \frac{40 - 20}{40} \text{ X } 41 = 20 \text{ g/100 liters}$$

Note that while chloride (Cl) is an essential *microelement*, it is not added to the formulation as it is present both in raw water and as a by-product of some of the other salts.

The pH of the nutrient solution should be checked and adjusted to 5.8–6.4, depending upon the plants grown, before the iron chelate is added.

Table 3: Nutrient Formulae

Crop	Compounds	g/100 liters (26 US gal.)	Elements Provided (ppm)	

A. MACROELEMENTS

Cucumbers (Seedlings 7–30 days):
    Part A.

	Calcium Nitrate	100	Ca ·	245
			N ·	172

    Part B.

	Potassium Nitrate	78	N ·	108
			K ·	302
	Magnesium Sulfate	41	Mg ·	40
			S ·	53
	Monopotassium Phosphate	20	P ·	45
			K ·	57

Cucumbers (31 days to maturity):
    Part A.

	Calcium Nitrate	82	Ca ·	200
			N ·	140

    Part B.

	Potassium Nitrate	78	N ·	108
			K ·	302
	Magnesium Sulfate	41	Mg ·	40
			S ·	53
	Monopotassium Phosphate	20	P ·	45
			K ·	57

Tomatoes (Seedlings to first fruit set—about 40 days):
    Part A.

	Calcium Nitrate	58	Ca ·	140
			N ·	98

    Part B.

	Potassium Nitrate	14	N ·	20
			K ·	56
	Magnesium Sulfate	31	Mg ·	30
			S ·	40
	Monopotassium Phosphate	25	P ·	55
			K ·	70
	Potassium Sulfate	39	K ·	174
			S ·	72

Table 3: Nutrient Formulae (continued)

Crop	Compounds	g/100 liters (26 US gal.)	Elements Provided (ppm)	

A. MACROELEMENTS

Tomatoes (41 days to maturity):
Part A.

| | Calcium Nitrate | 82 | Ca | 200 |
| | | | N | 140 |

Part B.

	Magnesium Sulfate	46	Mg	45
			S	60
	Monopotassium Phosphate	30	P	65
			K	83
	Potassium Sulfate	71	K	317
			S	131

Lettuce and Leafy Vegetables:
Part A.

| | Calcium Nitrate | 58 | Ca | 140 |
| | | | N | 98 |

Part B.

	Potassium Nitrate	29	N	42
			K	118
	Magnesium Sulfate	31	Mg	30
			S	40
	Monpotassium Phosphate	18	P	40
			K	51

B. MICROELEMENTS

	Compounds	g/100 liters	Elements
	Boric Acid	0.17	B · 0.3
	Manganese Sulfate	0.32	Mn · 0.8
	Copper Sulfate	0.028	Cu · 0.07
	Zinc Sulfate	0.045	Zn · 0.10
	Sodium Molybdate	0.013	Mo · 0.03
	Iron Chelate (10% iron)	3.0	Fe · 3.0

Preparation of the Nutrient Solution

Prepare the nutrient solution in the following sequence of steps, observing all precautions suggested by manufacturers of the various products.

1. Fill the nutrient solution tank with water to about one-third full.
2. Dissolve each fertilizer salt *separately* in a container of hot water.
3. Add potassium nitrate and potassium sulfate first to the nutrient solution tank.
4. Fill the solution tank to three-quarters full with water.
5. Next, add magnesium sulfate and monopotassium phosphate.
6. While slowly adding calcium nitrate, stir well.
7. Add all the *micro*nutrients except iron chelate.
8. Test and adjust the pH to 5.8–6.4.
9. Add the iron chelate and top-up the tank to final volume.

Often the home gardener growing hydroponically in small systems will require less than 100 liters (26 US gallons) of nutrient solution. For example, if only 10 liters of solution were to be made-up, the small amounts of fertilizers needed would be difficult to measure. Errors in weighing, associated with small quantities, can be reduced significantly as the amounts to be weighed are increased.

To do this, prepare concentrated stock solutions of the *mac*roelements of 100 times the strength of the final nutrient solution level. A supply of 100 liters of 100 times (100 X) strength stock solution is prepared and stored in a black, opaque, plastic garbage can. Three such tanks are needed to separately store parts A, B, and the microelement mixtures.

Table 4 summarizes the amounts of fertilizers to use for each stock solution. Weights for 100 liter, 50 liter (13.2 US gal.), and 19 liter (5 US gal.) tanks are given in the table.

The *micro*nutrient stock solution is prepared at 300 times final strength. In this way more accuracy can be achieved in weighing. The final nutrient solution is made by taking a proportionate volume measurement of each of the three stock solutions, using a graduated cylinder (available from scientific supply companies—see Appendix).

Table 4: Nutrient Stock Solutions

Crop	Compounds	Wt./100 l 26 US gal.	Wt./50 l 13 US gal.	Wt./19 l 5 US gal.
	A. Macroelements (100X)			
Cucumbers (Seedlings 7–30 days):				
Part A.				
	Calcium Nitrate	10.0 kg	5.0 kg	1.9 kg
Part B.				
	Potassium Nitrate	7.8 kg	3.9 kg	1.48 kg
	Magnesium Sulfate	4.1 kg	2.05 kg	779 g
	Monopotassium Phosphate	2.0 kg	1.0 kg	380 g
Cucumbers (31 days to maturity):				
Part A.				
	Calcium Nitrate	8.2 kg	4.1 kg	1.56 kg
Part B.				
	Potassium Nitrate	7.8 kg	3.9 kg	1.48 kg
	Magnesium Sulfate	4.1 kg	2.05 kg	779 g
	Monopotassium Phosphate	2.0 kg	1.0 kg	380 g
Tomatoes (Seedlings to first fruit set—about 40 days):				
Part A.				
	Calcium Nitrate	5.8 kg	2.9 kg	1.1 kg
Part B.				
	Potassium Nitrate	1.4 kg	700 g	266 g
	Magnesium Sulfate	3.1 kg	1.55 kg	589 g
	Monopotassium Phosphate	2.5 kg	1.25 kg	475 g
	Potassium Sulfate	3.9 kg	1.95 kg	741 g
Tomatoes (41 days to maturity):				
Part A.				
	Calcium Nitrate	8.2 kg	4.1 kg	1.56 kg
Part B.				
	Magnesium Sulfate	4.6 kg	2.3 kg	874 g
	Monopotassium Phosphate	3.0 kg	1.5 kg	570 g
	Potassium Sulfate	7.1 kg	3.55 kg	1.35 kg
Lettuce and Leafy Vegetables:				
Part A.				
	Calcium Nitrate	5.8 kg	2.9 kg	1.1 kg
Part B.				
	Potassium Nitrate	2.9 kg	1.45 kg	551 g
	Magnesium Sulfate	3.1 kg	1.55 kg	589 g
	Monopotassium Phosphate	1.8 kg	0.9 kg	342 g
	B. Microelements (300X)			
	Boric Acid	51.0 g	25.5 g	9.7 g
	Manganese Sulfate	96.0 g	48.0 g	18.2 g
	Copper Sulfate	8.4 g	4.2 g	1.6 g
	Zinc Sulfate	13.5 g	6.75 g	2.56 g
	Sodium Molybdate	3.9 g	1.95 g	0.74 g
	Iron Chelate (10% iron)	900.0 g	450.0 g	171.0 g

Note: Iron chelate is added last after adjusting the pH to 5.5–5.8.

Preparation of a nutrient solution from the concentrate: for example, 100 liters of nutrient solution for lettuce using the lettuce formulation is prepared as follows:

1. Fill the nutrient solution tank to about three-quarters full (75 liters for a 100 liter tank).
2. Measure a one liter volume of part A of the stock solution and mix it into the nutrient solution tank.
3. Mix one liter of stock solution B into the solution tank and stir well.
4. Fill the solution tank up to 90 liters with water, check and adjust the pH to 5.8–6.4.
5 Since the micronutrient stock solution is 300 times the final concentration, you need add only ⅓ of a liter (333 ml) of it to the nutrient solution tank.
6. Top up the nutrient tank to 100 liters with raw water.

If you are making 30 liters of final nutrient solution, the rates would be ³⁰⁄₁₀₀ or 30 percent of each stock solution volume:

Part A.   30 percent of 1 liter = 300 ml
Part B.   30 percent of 1 liter = 300 ml
Micro-Mix 30 percent of ⅓ liter = 111 ml

Top up the nutrient tank with water to 30 liters. Remember to always fill the nutrient tank to about three-quarters with raw water *before* adding any stock solutions to avoid precipitation of the compounds. Furthermore, always adjust the pH of the solu-tion as described below before adding the micronutrient mix.

pH and Electrical Conductivity (EC)

The pH value is a measure of acidity or alkalinity. The pH of the soil solution (nutrient solution) determines the availability to the plant roots of the various elements. A pH of less than 7 indicates acidity, 7 is neutral, and above 7 is basic (alkaline). Most plants prefer a pH level between 5.8 and 7.0, slightly acidic for optimum nutrient uptake.

Inorganic salts (fertilizers) dissolved in water diffuse (dissoci-ate) into individual electrically charged units called ions. These ions are available to plant roots in contact with the solution (soil or nutrient solution).

These ions in solution conduct an electric current. Con-ductance is expressed as a "Mho." Since such conductivity is relatively small, it is expressed as "milliMhos/cm," a measure-ment of conductivity through one cubic centimeter of solution.

The desired range is generally 2.0 to 4.0, depending on the stage of plant growth and vigor. Higher levels of electrical con-ductivity (EC) suppress vegetative growth, while lower to mid-dle levels promote growth. Thus, the EC should be raised in crops such as tomatoes and cucumbers as they begin fruiting, to slow vegetative growth and promote fruit development.

Electrical conductivity (EC) measures the conductance in a solution by all the minerals (solutes) dissolved in the solution; it does not differentiate among the various elements. Therefore, a solution may have an optimum EC but still be unbalanced. That is, the total dissolved solutes (TDS) are adequate, but the propor-tions of each solute might be incorrect for optimal growth. Hence, while EC is a good indicator of solution strength, it is still essential to renew the entire nutrient solution periodically. This is discussed in more detail later.

Conductivity meters are available in a price range from $50 to $500, depending upon their accuracy and sophistication. The inexpensive instruments are adequate for the home grower.

The accuracy of the instrument must be calibrated weekly with a standard solution (commercially available). If you wish, you can make up your own standard using calcium nitrate, one of the fertilizers needed in the nutrient solution, as follows:

> Mix a 0.1% solution and a 0.2% solution of calcium nitrate, using distilled water.
> 0.1% is 1,000 mg/liter or 1 g/liter. That is, one gram of calcium nitrate mixed in one liter of distilled water. This solution has a EC of 1.0 mMho.
> 0.2% is 2,000 mg/liter or 2 g/liter. This is, two grams of calcium nitrate mixed in one liter of distilled water. This solution has an EC of 2.0 mMho.

Electrical conductivity is discussed again in relation to individ-ual crop nutrition and nutrient solutions.

Adjustment of pH

The pH of the nutrient solution can be raised (made more basic) by use of potassium hydroxide (KOH), sodium hydroxide

(NaOH), or bicarbonate of soda ($NaHCO_3$). The latter is safest to use; the first two burn the skin.

Great caution must be observed, and goggles and rubber gloves must be worn when using the hydroxides (the first two compounds mentioned above). Carefully observe all of the cautions suggested by the manufacturer. The addition of small amounts (several grams) will quickly shift the pH of the nutrient solution toward basic.

A basic solution is lowered (made more acidic) by the addition of sulfuric adic (H_2SO_4)—battery acid; nitric acid (HNO_3); hydrochloric acid (HC1)—muriatic acid, sometimes used to treat swimming pools; or acetic acid, such as vinegar.

The best acid to use, from the standpoint of simple effectiveness, is sulfuric acid, but it is especially corrosive and—as with nitric acid and hydrochloric acid—burns the skin. So again, rubber gloves and goggles must be worn to prevent injury to hands and eyes.

Carefully observe all of the cautions suggested by the manufacturer when using this or any corrosive substance like acids or hydroxides.

It would be safer and easier to use vinegar in lowering the pH of your solution, even if larger amounts are needed than with the stronger acids.

Never add water to acid, but add acid to water or to the nutrient solution to prevent splashing.

You do not need to purchase a sophisticated, expensive pH meter. Such meters are difficult to maintain in calibration. A simpler, and adequate, method is to use indicator (litmus) paper, or an indicator solution as is found in swimming pool pH test kits.

Be sure to use indicator papers or solutions that test in the pH range from 5.0 to 7.5, preferably in increments of 0.1 pH units.

CHAPTER 3 | # *Backyard Greenhouses*

A backyard greenhouse makes it possible for you to do really serious and productive hydroponic gardening.

Select a backyard greenhouse equipped with one or several hydroponic systems.

Location in your backyard, site preparation, electrical needs, and environmental control components are important factors in determining the nature of the structure, its size, and the costs.

The hydroponic system and its arrangement within the greenhouse is discussed and well illustrated.

Home greenhouses are diverse in materials, shapes, and sizes to suit the tastes of most backyard gardeners.

For a conventional 8- by 10-foot (2.4m × 3.65 m) structure, prices vary from $200 to $300 for wood-polyethylene to $3,000 or more for aluminum-glass models. Your choice depends upon the amount of annual usage you expect from it and how many years you expect to garden.

For the really serious gardener I recommend either a aluminum-framed fiberglass or glass structure. Life expectancy of such structures is 20 to 30 years. But less expensive structures can give long and satisfying service.

I was once a partner in a greenhouse manufacturing company that specialized in backyard greenhouses and hydroponics, so I will discuss components relating to the aluminum-fiberglass structures that are commonly available. Most of our houses were purchased with a trickle-feed, gravel culture system. The elements discussed here are similar to those found in many other kinds of systems.

Before you decide on purchasing a greenhouse, check out a few factors related to your backyard and home.

First, even an expensive greenhouse, fully equipped with a hydroponic system, cannot grow a satisfactory crop of vegetables if your yard is shaded from direct sunlight by tall trees belonging to you or your neighbours. Your greenhouse must be located in a sunny area in your yard. You can always reduce sunlight in the summer months, if necessary, by applying to the greenhouse a type of white-wash shading compound, removing it in the early fall months.

Second, be sure that your home has sufficient electrical power. Since the supplemental heating used in most backyard greenhouses is electrical, you will need 30–60 amperes of power to run the greenhouse, depending on your climate. That means your home should ideally have a 200-amp service, with some spare circuits available for the greenhouse. If not, you may want to have your electrical system upgraded by an electrician—not a bad idea anyway in most older homes.

If everything checks out and you purchase or build a do-it-yourself greenhouse, prepare the site where it is to be constructed. Remember, in locating the greenhouse, the farther it is from your electrical main box, the more underground wiring you will have to purchase.

Prepare the site by placing treated rough cedar, 2- by 4-inch sills on edge, defining a rectangle one foot wider than the greenhouse perimeter. That is, for a 10- by 12-foot greenhouse, prepare a base that measures 12 by 14 feet.

Stake the sills in place, being sure that they are square—by making the diagonal measurements equal. Place the stakes on the inside and in the corners. After levelling the sills, nail the stakes to them.

Treat the cedar with a wood preservative like cuprinol (copper napthanate). Do not use pentachlorophenol as its fumes are toxic to plants—and other living things. If in doubt, paint the sills to help preserve the wood. Be sure to read and follow manufacturers' directions and cautions with respect to any materials you may use for this purpose.

Cover the inside ground surface and the sills with 6-mil black polyethylene. Make some slits in the bottom to allow drainage.

With the help of a licensed electrician, run approved underground electrical cable from your house to the pad end where the greenhouse control center is to be located. This cable should be buried at least one foot deep, or whatever depth is specified by your local building codes. You may be required to have the cable in a hard conduit. Be sure that the cable does not run across a garden where you roto-till or where digging may take place. Post appropriate signs with warnings about the underground wire.

Fill the pad area with pea gravel, this is especially convenient if you are installing a gravel culture system (fig. 56) in the first place. You may later place concrete stepping stones or board walks between your beds after the greenhouse has been completed (figs. 57, 58).

Many greenhouses are prefabricated so you can easily erect them with the help of one other person.

We built our greenhouses with complete gable ends. One end contained an aluminum glass door installed before delivery. The first step was to attach the gable ends, on their own sills, to the side sills with aluminum brackets (fig. 59). Everything was screwed or bolted together so that the houses could be disassembled for moving.

The fiberglass was attached to the aluminum-framed gable ends by pop rivets. The aluminum ribs and purlins (horizontal members) were bolted loosely with stainless steel bolts. The sills were squared and levelled before tightening the bolts. Once these bolts were tightened, the greenhouse became a rigid structue (fig. 60).

High quality (10-year guarantee) corrugated fiberglass was attached under the ridge piece and bent down to the sill where it was fastened with aluminum nails (fig. 61, 62). A foam closure strip between the fiberglass corrugations and sill sealed all outside air from entering the house (fig. 63). Several pop rivets fasten the fiberglass to each of the purlins (fig. 64). Once all the fiberglass was on, the ridge cap was tightened down with closure strips sealing the fiberglass at the top (fig. 65). Finally, the fiberglass overhang at each gable end was caulked with silicone rubber sealant (fig. 66).

Figure 56. A site pad filled with pea gravel prepared as a base for a 10½- by 12-foot backyard greenhouse.

Figure 57. A 10½- by 12-foot aluminum framed, fiberglass greenhouse with a pea gravel culture, trickle irrigation system. Note the placement of stepping stones and a boardwalk around and within the greenhouse. *Courtesy of Resh Greenhouses Ltd., Vancouver, B.C.*

Figure 58. The interior arrangement of growing beds, nutrient tank, control panel, fan, and louvres of a 10½- by 12- foot greenhouse.

Figure 59. Constructing an 8- by 12-foot backyard greenhouse. Fiberglass gable ends are attached to treated cedar sills. *Courtesy of Resh Greenhouses Ltd., Vancouver, B.C.*

Figure 60. Purlins (horizontal members) are attached to the vertical ribs and the house is squared and levelled. *Courtesy of Resh Greenhouses Ltd., Vancouver, B.C.*

Figure 61. Corrugated fiberglass is attached under the ridge purlin and bent down to the sill. *Courtesy of Resh Greenhouses Ltd., Vancouver, B.C.*

Figure 62. Corrugated fiberglass is attached to the sill by aluminum nails. Note the two cross members on the front gable to support the beds. *Courtesy of Resh Greenhouses Ltd., Vancouver, B.C.*

Figure 63. Closure strips are pressed between the fiberglass and sill as the fiberglass is nailed to the sill. This seals the greenhouse from outside air.

101

Figure 64. Pop rivets attach the fiberglass panels to the ribs in several places. *Courtesy of Resh Greenhouses Ltd., Vancouver, B.C.*

Figure 65. The author placing closure strips under the ridge purlin (cross member) to seal the fiberglass panels. *Courtesy of Resh Greenhouses Ltd., Vancouver, B.C.*

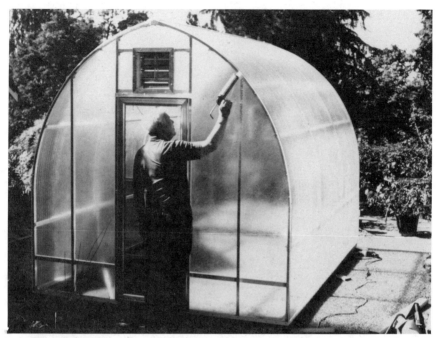

Figure 66. The gable ends and end fiberglass panels are sealed with silicone rubber where they overlap. *Courtesy of Resh Greenhouses Ltd., Vancouver, B.C.*

Figure 67. Tucked into a small backyard, here is the completed 8- by 12-foot greenhouse with hydroponic beds. Note the beds are supported by the end brackets on the gables. A styrofoam insulation was installed on the side walls between the beds and wall to reduce heat loss next to the beds. The height of the insulation was only to the top of the beds so as not to shade the plants.

Figure 68. A 10½- by 16-foot backyard greenhouse having three different culture methods. The left bed uses plastic, 5-gallon pots filled with pea gravel, the center beds are a NFT (Nutrient film technique) system, and the bed on the right uses pea gravel with a trickle feed system. *Courtesy of Resh Greenhouses Ltd., Vancouver, B.C.*

Figure 69. A 10½- by 16-foot aluminum-framed, fiberglass greenhouse. Note the insulated lower walls. *Courtesy of Resh Greenhouses Ltd.*

Figure 70. An 8- by 12-foot lean-to, aluminum-fiberglass greenhouse. *Courtesy of Resh Greenhouses Ltd., Vancouver, B.C.*

Figure 71. An 8- by 16-foot lean-to greenhouse constructed against a fence. *Courtesy of Resh Greenhouses Ltd., Vancouver, B.C.*

The exhaust fan is screwed into the rear gable end and caulked. Generally, the inlet shutters on the opposite end are installed by the manufacturer. An electrical control panel and the pump header piping was installed on the rear gable end (figs. 58, 67).

The hydroponic system was set up next.

The fiberglass nutrient solution tank was set against the rear gable wall perpendicular to the beds (fig. 50). Setting the tank slightly into the gravel pad base levels it securely.

The beds are sloped two inches back towards the nutrient tank (fig. 50).

The gable ends were fitted with an aluminum channel cross-support to hold the beds at the correct slope. The beds at the same time held down the greenhouse. A column of concrete blocks set under the center of each bed provided further support as the gravel medium was very heavy.

Alternatives to gravel culture include the nutrient film technique or rockwool systems (fig. 68), using smaller beds. The beds would be arranged *above* the nutrient reservoir, positioned in a similar manner, at the same slope as for gravel culture.

The nutrient tank in the system I have been describing, contained either a submersible pump or sump pump, connected via a header pipe to a trickle feed system (fig. 51). This same design would be appropriate for rockwool culture.

The nutrient tank was kept dark by plywood covers.

The heater was placed on one of the tank covers (fig. 51).

Fastened to the rear gable end was a fully wired control panel with all electrical outlets (fig. 51). It contained one time-clock to operate the pump and another for controlling supplementary lights.

Three 8-foot, cool-white, high output fluorescent lights were suspended in the greenhouse by jack chains (fig. 51). One light was positioned above each growing bed. The jack chains facilitated the raising of the lights as the crop grew higher.

The control panel was wired with a main breaker to which the underground cable from the gardener's home was attached (fig. 51).

When an exhaust fan was activated by a thermostat for cooling, the negative pressure created in the greenhouse opened the intake louvers on the front gable.

You may find greenhouses available in several basic, free-standing models, similar to those we offered: 8 by 12 feet, 10½ by 12 feet, 10½ by 16 feet, and 10½ by 20 feet. The most popular model was the 10½- by 12-foot size. Also, several lean-to models, for use against a building wall, of 8 by 12 feet and 8 by 16 feet, were manufactured (figs. 57, 67, 68, 69, 70, 71).

Most backyard gardeners can grow a combination of crops, including lettuce, Swiss chard, parsley, watercress, basil, tomatoes, and cucumbers. A 10½- by 12-foot greenhouse could produce 1,000 pounds (455 kg) of tomaotes, 2,000 cucumbers, or 1,000 head of lettuce annually, or a combination of crops, such as 400 pounds (180 kg) of tomatoes, 700 cucumbers and 400 lettuce (figs. 53-55, 72, 73).

A hobby greenhouse is not usually purchased for the economics of its productivity alone. It offers welcome relief from daily stress. It produces healthful food of high quality and superior flavor rarely available today from the supermarket. It provides useful relaxation and, at the same time, is an interesting and challenging hobby.

Figure 72. Ripe tomatoes ready to harvest. *Figure 73.* Tomatoes and cucumbers grown in pea gravel of a backyard greenhouse.

CHAPTER 4 | # Caring for Your Plants

This chapter tells you about the optimum environmental conditions under which to grow plants and how to control those conditions.

Also: how to propagate your seedlings, and how to choose the most suitable plant varieties for hydroponic systems.

You will also learn about spacing for various kinds of plants, training, pruning, and pollinating, with illustrated step-by-step procedures to teach you the best cultural practices that will insure success in your hydroponic garden.

And you will learn how to avoid problems through an awareness of symptoms, identification of pests, and the application of natural pest controls.

Environmental Conditions

As mentioned earlier, hydroponics virtually guarantees you successful growing—if you provide plants with the correct environmental conditions!

Light

Proper light levels and temperatures influence plant growth. Light quality, intensity, and duration determine productivity of plants.

The best light is natural sunlight for a period of 12 to 16 hours daily, with a dark period of about 8 hours, for most vegetables. During darkness, respiration takes place in the building of tissues, reproductive structures, and other metabolic activities.

Supplementary artificial light, from cool-white, high output fluorescent or high intensity discharge sodium vapor lamps, is beneficial to plants when sunlight is unavailable, but it is not a complete substitution. Intensity of supplementary lighting should be about 800–1,000 foot-candles at the plant surface. Supplementary lighting is particularly useful for extending daylength to 14–16 hours during winter months.

Light should be prevented from entering the nutrient solution, as it promotes algae growth. Use opaque containers with covers for nutrient reservoirs and opaque white, grey, or black plastic piping to conduct the nutrient solution.

Temperature

Temperature must be maintained at optimum levels for your plants. In a backyard greenhouse you must provide heating in cold weather and cooling in hot weather. A thermostatically controlled heater and exhaust fan are ideal for this. Even during some summer nights, the temperature dips below optimum levels, so heating may be necessary if you want to keep plants growing.

During sunlight conditions the greenhouse traps heat through the "greenhouse effect" by admitting short wave radiation from the sun but confining long wave radiation from the greenhouse interior. The long wave rays cannot readily escape, and therefore the temperature rises quickly.

An exhaust fan must be large enough to exchange the air volume of the greenhouse every 30 seconds. This rate of air exchange will keep temperatures within 5 degrees of ambient.

Under high light conditions during the summer it may be beneficial to reduce the transmissibility of the greenhouse by 25 percent through the application of a greenhouse shading compound. It can be applied with a paint sprayer. This slight reduction in light will reduce the heat build-up, yet will not decrease the light below optimum levels. The compound must be washed off by early fall as sunlight intensity decreases.

Smaller indoor hydroponic units should be provided with supplementary artificial lighting, even if they are located in front of a large, south-facing window. Unless the sunlight reaches the plants for at least 12 hours per day, supplementary lighting will assist growing. Even so, daylength can be extended to 14–16 hours with the lights.

pH and EC

Another significant factor in determining your indoor garden-ing success is how well you maintain optimum nutrient levels. This is done by monitoring the pH (acidity/alkalinity) and EC (electrical conductivity).

As outlined earlier, the availability of essential elements to plants is pH-dependent. Generally, the solution's pH should be between 5.8 and 6.5 depending upon the specific plants grown. As discussed earlier (in Chapter 2) you may adjust the pH down-wards (more acidic) by addition of an acid and upwards (more basic) by addition of a base. Common household vinegar and bicarbonate of soda can be used for this purpose.

Electrical conductivity of the solution, easily measured by a conductivity meter, is more difficult to regulate. Since EC simply measures the total nutrient level, it is not possible to determine which elements may be out of proportion.

It does, however, tell you whether or not sufficient total ele-ments are present. Therefore, you may adjust all the elements upwards by a percentage equal to the EC's percentage decline from optimum as discussed in Chapter 2. If the EC continues to fall each week, you must change the whole nutrient solution to correct the imbalances in individual nutrients. As a rule, the nutrient solution should be replaced completely anyway every four to five weeks to avoid nutrient imbalances.

Growing Seedlings

There are a number of options in starting your plants. Most vegetables are started from seed. Herbs can initially be started as seeds followed by cuttings rooted from parent plants for suc-cessive generations.

Your choice of seeding method is somewhat dependent upon the type of hydroponic system. For example, use small rockwool blocks for planting in rockwool, sawdust, and NFT cultures (figs. 26–28, 74). Use peat pellets for sand, gravel, peat-lite mixes, vermiculite, and perlite cultures. "Com-pack" trays in flats with a vegetable plug mix are suitable for growing leafy vegetables in NFT, water culture, and peat-lite mixtures.

Figure 74. Cucumbers germinated in rockwool cubes and transplanted to rockwool blocks after 5 days.

Larger seeds of plants like tomatoes, cucumbers, melons, and peppers should be pressed into the medium about ¼-inch deep. Rockwool blocks must be thoroughly soaked with a half-strength nutrient solution prior to seeding.

Place the rockwool blocks or peat pellets in flats prior to sowing the seeds. Be sure flats have drainage holes. After sowing, cover the seed holes with vermiculite before moistening again.

Peat pellets are compressed peat discs covered with a nylon mesh (fig. 52). Soak the pellets in water for 5–10 minutes until they swell to about 1½ inches (4 cm) in height and are completely soft throughout. Push the seeds about ¼-inch into the medium with a pencil and cover them with the surrounding peat. Peat pellets have sufficient nutrients to carry the plants for three to four weeks.

When sowing into a vegetable plug mix in "Com-pack" trays and flats, pre-moisten the medium slightly before placing it in the trays. Press the medium ¼-inch into the tray with a dibbler before sowing. Cover the seeds with additional medium, press slightly, then water the seeds in. Sow at least two seeds per block or pellet for most vegetables (use one seed per cube for cucumbers and melons).

It is helpful to cover each tray with a sheet of black polyethylene to maintain moisture until germination occurs. Immediately upon germination, remove the plastic cover and set the seedlings in the light, or as they extend, they will become very spindly.

As soon as the seedlings reach cotyledon state (showing the first "leaf" or pair of "leaves"), cut the less vigorous ones out with scissors, right down to the top of the cube in which they are growing, leaving one plant in each cube. If this is not done at an early stage, the seedlings will become spindly as they compete for light.

Temperatures during germination should be about 65°F. (18°C) at night and 75°F. (24°C) during the day. If the temperatures are too low, plant growth will be slowed and "damping-off" (fungus disease) of seedlings becomes more likely. If temperatures are too high, plants will be soft and "leggy." Optimum temperatures for vine crops are about 65°F. (18°C) at night and not greater than 85°F. (29°C) during the day.

Table 5: Crop Spacing

Crop	Plant Spacing		Aisle Spacing	Type of Culture	Type of Rows
	Within Rows	Between Rows			
Cucumbers and Melons	20″ (50cm)	36″ (91cm)	60″ (152cm)	Rockwool, Peat Mixes, Sawdust, Sand, Gravel	Double
Tomatoes, Peppers	20″ (50cm)	24″ (61cm)	30″ (76cm)	Rockwool, Peat Mixes, Sawdust, Sand, Gravel	Double
Lettuce, Herbs, Leafy Vegetables	7″ (18cm)	8″ (20cm)	None	NFT Raceway	Single 4 or More

Table 6: Vegetable Varieties Suitable to Hydroponics.

Vegetable	Varieties
Cucumbers-European	Toska 70, Pandex, Farbio, Sandra, Corona, Marillo, Fidelio
Tomatoes (staking)	Tropic, Dombito, Caruso, Larma, Perfecto, Laura
Peppers (bell-types)	
Green to red, use:	Delphin, Plutona, Tango
Green to yellow, use:	Luteus, Goldstar
Lettuce-European	Deci-Minor, Ostinata, Satonia, Buttercrunch
Looseleaf	Domineer, Grand Rapids, Black-Seeded Simpson, Waldmann's Dark Green

Transplanting, Spacing

Seedlings should be respaced at least once before transplanting. This generally will be after the third and fourth true leaves unfold. They should be spaced before the leaves of adjacent plants overlap. A spacing of about 6 by 6 inches (16 cm by 15 cm) will be sufficient.

Good, sturdy transplants will grow to become healthy plants (fig. 75). Handle seedlings carefully to avoid damaging roots or shoots. Rough handling will result in growth "set-back" during transplanting and a greater possibility of diseases.

Transplant after the seedlings have 3–4 true leaves and their roots penetrate the growing cubes.

Under bright, sunny conditions it is best to transplant in the evening so that the seedlings have time to root into the new medium overnight before undergoing water stress the next day.

Plant spacing must be sufficient to allow proper training and adequate light to reach the crop. Vine crops are placed in double rows per bed, while leafy crops are spaced to utilize as much floor area as possible. If leafy vegetables or herbs are grown in single rows, such as in the NFT system, the rows should be spaced 7 to 8 inches (18 to 20 cm) apart, with the plants spaced the same distance apart within rows. In a raceway culture system, plants are spaced 7 inches (18 cm) by 8 inches (20 cm) over the entire bed surface (fig. 76).

A summary of plant spacing for some crops is given in Table 5.

Training, Pruning, Pollinating, Harvesting

Vine crops are trained vertically onto plastic string. In rock-wool and sawdust cultures, using rockwool propagation blocks, you may place the lower end of the string between the slab (or bag) and the growing block (fig. 30). As the roots grow into the underlying material, they will anchor the end of the string. This will eliminate the need to use plastic vine clips or the tying of the string to the base of the plant.

After three to four days as the plant becomes established, start wrapping the string around the stem. Always go in one direction (preferably clockwise) to eliminate any confusion in future string-ing. Try to get one wind between each set of leaves. (fig. 77)

If the plant slips down the string as it becomes laden with fruit, place a plastic clip under a leaf axil (fig. 78).

Figure 75. Mature European seedless cucumbers growing in rockwool. Note the trickle irrigation system. *Courtesy of Environmental Farms, Dundee, Florida.*

Figure 76. Mature European lettuce (about 32 days from transplanting) growing in a raceway water culture system. *Courtesy of Hoppmann Hydroponics, Waverly, Florida.*

Figure 77. Winding support string around a cucumber plant in a clockwise direction. The small cucumber is about 6 inches (15 cm) long (3–4 days after initial swelling).

Clip Hinge

Support String

Figure 78. A plant clip placed under a leaf supports a tomato plant.

These plant clips are available in two sizes (¾-inch and 1-inch diameters) from greenhouse suppliers. Use the ¾-inch diameter clips for tomatoes and the 1-inch diameter clips for the thicker-stemmed cucumbers. Be sure to place the string *in the hinge* of the plastic clip to prevent slipping.

Tomatoes, cucumbers, and peppers must be pruned to vertical form. As each crop requires somewhat different training, the procedures for each are discussed in detail separately. To take advantage of limited space in a backyard greenhouse or indoor patio use staking (climbing) tomato varieties rather than bush varieties. In smaller, indoor hydroponic units, it may be easier to use a bush tomato and change the crop more often. Generally, a staking greenhouse variety is used (see Table 6 for recommended varieties).

Tomatoes

Tomatoes are pruned to a single stem supported by a stake or string (fig. 79). Stringing is most convenient in a greenhouse or patio where support cables can be strung above the crop to which the strings may be fastened. In smaller growing units a lath trellis could be used.

The suckers (shoots) between the main stem and each leaf petiole are removed early when one inch (2.5 cm) in length (fig. 80). The larger they grow, the more nutrients they take from the plant, the larger the scars left on breaking, and the more difficult they are to break. Break them off by grasping them between the thumb and forefinger of one hand while holding the plant stem directly below the sucker with the other hand. This will prevent bruising or breaking the main stem as you snap off the sucker.

It is better to remove the side shoots by hand than with a knife, as a knife spreads diseases more readily. You may wear rubber or disposable plastic gloves to protect your hands from the stains of the acidic plant sap.

If a plant loses its growing point by breakage, or naturally, allow a vigorous side shoot near the growing point to continue growing. Often plants fork at the top. Simply remove the less vigorous shoot, allowing the other to continue.

Lower leaves which start yellowing as the plant reaches 4 to 5 feet (120 to 150 cm) in height, should be removed to give better air circulation to the plant base, thus reducing humidity. Continue removing yellow lower leaves up to the ripening fruit as the

Figure 79. Tomato plant supported by a string and plant clip. Note the fruit cluster has been pruned to 4 flowers. Suckers have been removed from leaf axils.

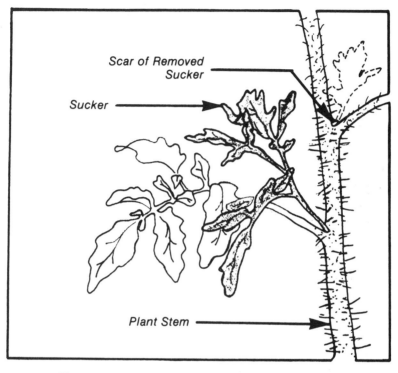

Figure 80. Removal of tomato suckers from leaf axils.

plant matures. Snap off the leaves by hand to get a clean break next to the stem. Remove all suckers and leaves from the growing area.

When the plants reach the horizontal support cables above, lower the plants several feet by loosening the vertical support string. (When stringing always leave three to four feet extra of string beyond the upper cable). Because the lower leaves and fruit have been removed earlier, the stems can be lowered along the top of the bed (fig. 81). Four to five feet (120 to 150 cm) of foliage should remain on the plant at all times.

Allow no more than four to five flowers on each truss (cluster of flowers). Remove misshapen flowers, double-set fruit, and often the furthest one out in the truss. This fruit pruning will result in more uniform size, shape and color of tomatoes (fig. 80). It should be done as soon as small fruit (¼-inch diameter) set.

Tomatoes must be pollinated by hand. You may tap the flower cluster with your finger or vibrate it with an electric vibrator (available at greenhouse suppliers). Under favorable environmental conditions you will see a fine yellow pollen flowing from the flower upon vibration. Flowers are receptive (ready for pollination) when their petals curl backwards. Pollination should be done at least every other day between 11:00 AM and 3:00 PM when there is the most light and the lowest relative humidity. Effective pollination will result in small bead-like fruit development within a week. This is termed fruit-set.

Cucumbers

European cucumbers are trained in one of two ways: the renewal umbrella system (fig. 82) or the V-cordon system (fig. 83). In the V-cordon system, two support wires about 7 feet (2.1 m) above the ground, spaced 3 feet (90 cm) apart are located above each row of plants. Support strings are located above each row of plants. Support strings are tied alternately to the overhead wires so that the plants are inclined away from the row on each side.

Suckers and fruit are removed from the plants up to the fifth leaf to reduce stress on the plant as it becomes established. If this is not done, fruit will abort and plant vigor will be slowed; there would be insufficient nutrients to develop them. Thin any multiple fruits in leaf axils to one and remove all tendrils, they wind around leaves, fruit, and stems, causing distortion and scars.

Figure 81. As lower leaves of tomatoes are removed, the plants are lowered. Stems are bent along the growing bed.

Figure 82. Renewal umbrella system of training European cucumbers.

The renewal umbrella system of training is the most popular method. One support wire at 7 feet (2.1 m) is placed above each row of plants. The rows are spaced 3 feet (90 cm) apart. An extra support wire is positioned 2 feet (60 cm) into the aisle from each row of plants. The renewal laterals are placed along this wire and allowed to hang down into the aisle 3–4 feet (1 m).

The training procedure is as follows:

1. Prune all suckers to the wire.
2. Remove all tendrils on the entire plant.
3. Prune all fruit from the main stem up to the seventh node (leaf axil).
4. Allow one fruit to develop at the eighth node, then skip two nodes, allowing one fruit.
5. Allow every other fruit to develop to the wire beginning at the tenth to eleventh node. This should leave about 6–7 stem fruit in total.
6. The main stem should be stopped at one leaf above the support wire. Pinch out the growing point at that level. Tie a small loop of string around the wire and below the top leaf or use a plant clip under the second from top leaf to prevent the plant from sliding down the main string.

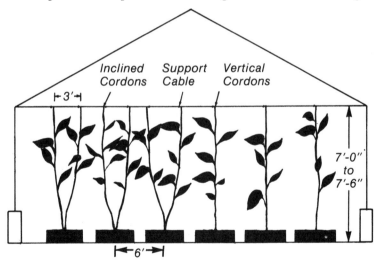

Figure 83. V-cordon system of training European cucumbers.

7. Train the top two laterals over the wire and onto the second support wire, the one above the aisle.
8. Remove all secondary laterals on the main stem except two at the top.
9. While the fruit on the first lateral are maturing, let the next first lateral grow out and along the wire. Remove the rest of the shoots from the main laterals.
10. When the laterals fall about 3 feet (1 m) below the second wire, into the aisle, cut off the tip.
11. When the fruits on the first lateral have been harvested, remove it completely or to within 6 inches (15 cm) of the aisle support wire, allowing the next first lateral to develop.
12. Remove three leaves from the top of the plant between the support wires to get more light into the crop.
13. Continued renewal of the system is achieved by repeating steps 9 through 12 above.

The better European cucumber varieties (see Table 6) are all female, so no pollination is required. In fact, pollination must be avoided in order to get seedless cucumbers. The more recent all-female varieties have no male flowers so pollination will not occur.

Similarly to tomatoes, as the cucumber vine grows towards the support cables, their lower leaves will senesce (turn yellow) from mutual shading. Remove all yellowing leaves to allow better air circulation at the plant base. Leaves must be cut with a sharp razor or pruning shears. They cannot be snapped off by hand as was the case with tomatoes. Cut them within ¼-inch of the stem.

Such pruning is best done in the late morning or early afternoon when lower relative humidity will favor quick drying of the wound, to prevent diseases. Suckering and winding of the plants up the support string is easier during the afternoon when the plant is less turgid. Otherwise, stems break easily. If side shoots and tendrils are small, they can be snapped off carefully by hand as was described for tomatoes. Larger suckers and tendrils must be cut off with pruning shears or a razor blade.

Fruit is harvested from the plant by cutting the fruit stem with pruning shears close (within 2 mm) to the fruit shoulder. Harvest in the late morning or early afternoon when the plants are dry. Fruit are ready to harvest when they are about 1½ inches (4 cm) in diameter or slightly larger. Fruit color should be a dark green; no yellowing should be apparent. Length should be a minimum of

12 inches (30 cm). Any misshapen fruit (curled) is normally removed during early growth. The home gardener can eat these small fruit; they are crisp and flavorful.

Peppers

Peppers should be transplanted when the first (crown) flower bud appears. This will be about five to six weeks after sowing the seed. To encourage initial vegetative growth, remove the flower buds from the first and second leaf axils. That is, remove the flower buds from the first 16 inches (40 cm) of growth. Peppers bifurcate (fork) at each axil where flower buds form.

Several methods of training plants are commonly practiced. One technique is to allow all shoots to grow, and the plants are supported by horizontal nets. Another is partial suckering while training the plants up strings.

With the stringing method, train two leaders per plant up separate strings (fig. 84). Fasten the base of each string to the plant with a plastic vine clip as described earlier for tomatoes. Wrap the vine around the string in a clockwise directions. Soft-pinch out the side shoots at their second leaf axil. Fruit will form in each axil (fig. 85). In this way, each side shoot should produce two fruit. Continue this training to the overhead support wire, then terminate the plant by pinching out the growing point.

Peppers are very delicate, so you must be careful not to break the shoots, leaves, or fruit while training them.

With the horizontal net system of training, nets of 8-inch-square (20 cm) mesh are installed every 14 inches (30 cm) or so, and upward, with the first one positioned about 24 inches (60cm) above the floor. Picking is more difficult with the net system and the risk of disease is greater due to the high relative humidity that the nets tend to retain in the crop canopy.

Most bell-type sweet peppers are green, ripening to either red or yellow (fig. 86). Peppers may be picked as mature green peppers or they must be allowed to fully ripen red or yellow. It takes about 6 weeks after the mature green stage to turn color.

To harvest, simply break the fruit away from the stalk by hand. The peduncle (stalk) should remain attached to the fruit after harvesting or shelf life is greatly reduced. To avoid breaking the stems it is better to harvest in the afternoon when the plant is more flexible.

Lettuce, spinach, and many herbs do not require any special training. In general, herbs should be kept pruned back so that

Figure 84. Peppers trained as two leaders.

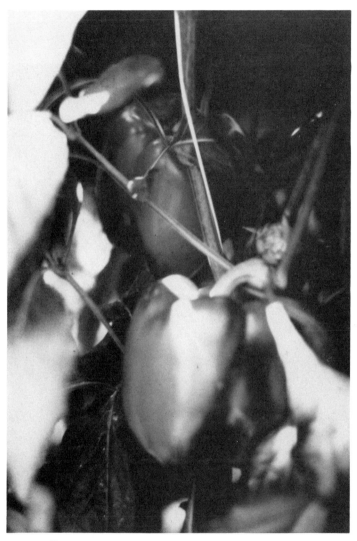

Figure 85. Peppers produce fruit at each leaf axil.

Figure 86. Yellow peppers just harvested.

renewed young growth is always present. If you are interested in growing herbs, purchase a book on their specific cultural requirements. *Artistically Cultivated Herbs* (Woodbridge Press) is an interesting example.

Vegetable Varieties

When growing indoors you should use greenhouse varieties of vegetables. A summary of the more popular varieties suitable to hydroponics is given in Table 6, repeated here for your convenience.

Table 6: Vegetable Varieties Suitable to Hydroponics.

Vegetable	Varieties
Cucumbers-European	Toska 70, Pandex, Farbio, Sandra, Corona, Marillo, Fidelio
Tomatoes (staking)	Tropic, Dombito, Caruso, Larma, Perfecto, Laura
Peppers (bell-types)	
Green to red, use:	Delphin, Plutona, Tango
Green to yellow, use:	Luteus, Goldstar
Lettuce-European	Deci-Minor, Ostinata, Satonia, Buttercrunch
Looseleaf	Domineer, Grand Rapids, Black-Seeded Simpson, Waldmann's Dark Green

Nutritional Disorders, Diseases, and Insect Pests

It is important to note some problems related to environmental conditions (physiological disorders). These disorders are defects caused by nonoptimal temperatures, poor nutrition (imbalances of nutrient levels, or pH), or improper irrigation.

The following is a list of disorders common to tomatoes, peppers, and cucumbers:

1. Blossom-end rot (tomatoes, peppers) (fig. 87)—a brown leathery tissue at the blossom end of the fruit.
   Cause: calcium deficiency, water stress due to insufficient irrigation frequency, or poor root aeration.
2. *Fruit cracking* (tomatoes) (fig. 88)—cracks radiating from the stem on maturing fruits.
   Cause: infrequent water cycles, high temperatures.
3. *Blotchy ripening* (tomatoes)—uneven fruit coloring, brown areas inside fruit.
   Cause: low light intensity, cool temperatures, high nitrogen.
4. *Green shoulder, sunscald* (tomatoes)—green blotches on fruit, uneven ripening.
   Cause: high temperatures and light striking fruit.
   Remedy: do not prune leaves above ripening fruit.
5. *Catfacing* (tomatoes) (fig. 89)—distortion of fruit, protuberances on face.
   Cause: poor pollination due to low light, high relative humidity.
6. *Crooking* (cucumbers) (fig. 90)—excessive fruit curvature.
   Cause: fruit hanging up on a stem, leaf, or tendrils during its expansion.
7. *Abortion of fruit* (cucumbers, peppers)—fruit yellows and dries up while still small.
   Cause: too heavy a fruit load, poor nutrition, low light, improper training.

Plants grown indoors are susceptible to certain common pests and diseases. Vigilance and early identification are important in controlling such problems.

A number of books and government publications are available on identification and control of pests. More information and illustrations appear in *Hydroponic Food Production* (Woodbridge Press), see Appendix.

Figure 87. Blossom-end rot of tomatoes.

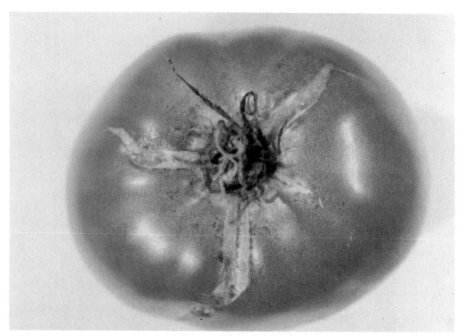

Figure 88. Fruit cracking of tomatoes.

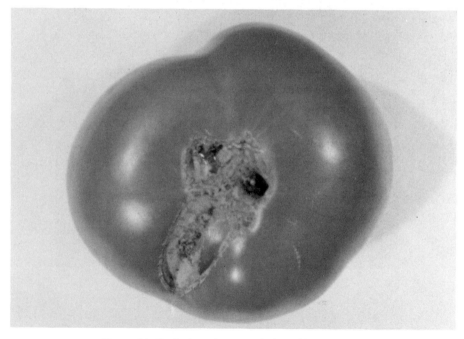

Figure 89. Catfacing of tomato fruit on blossom end.

Figure 90. Crooking of cucumber fruit.

Some common tomato diseases:

1. *Leaf mold* (fig. 91)—starts as small gray spot on undersides of leaves, expanding to pale areas. It is often associated with the presence of sucking insects.

   Control: eliminate insects, prevent high humidity

2. *Wilt*—Plants initially wilt on hot days, then, as disease progresses, plants wilt permanently as the roots die.

   Control: sterilization between crops.

3. *Gray mold*—under high humidity, wounds and scars develop a watery rot with fluffy gray growth.

   Control: reduce humidity, use fungicides, remove badly infected plants.

4. *Virus* (fig. 92)—distortion of leaves, stunting of growth.

   Control: remove infected plants, eliminate sucking insects, use resistant varieties.

Some common cucumber diseases:

1. *Powdery mildew* (fig. 93)—white spots appear on upper surface of leaves and spread rapidly, resulting in a "snowy" white appearance as spots expand and coalesce.

   Control: lower relative humidity by ventilation, resistant varieties, use fungicides.

2. *Cucumber mosaic virus*—dwarfed leaves, discolored, distorted leaves.

   Control: remove plants and wash hands with soap and water to prevent spreading it.

3. *Gray mold*—same as for tomatoes.

Insects of tomatoes, cucumbers and peppers:

1. *Whitefly*—usually located on undersides of leaves, has a triangular white body, secretes a "honeydew" sticky substance on the leaves; later a black fungus often develops as a secondary infection.

   Control: eliminate insects by use of insecticides or a biological control agent (predatory wasp).

2. *Two-spotted spider mite* (fig. 94)—particularly common on cucumbers. Use a magnifying glass to observe the mites—they have a dark spot on each side of the body. As infestation increases, leaves become yellow with many small pin-sized dots coalescing, webbing appears on undersides of leaves.

   Control: use insecticides such as "Vendex" or a biological agent (predatory mite).

3. *Aphids*—form in clusters (colonies) on leaf undersides and on succulent new growth. Aphids may be green, black or brown, pear-shaped body, excrete "honeydew."
   Control: use insecticides or biological agents such as lady beetles or green lacewings.
4. *Leafminer* (fig. 95)—larvae eat "tunnels" inside leaves between the upper and lower epidermis.
   Control: use insecticides or biological agents.
5. *Caterpillars and cutworms*—brown or green worm-like larvae chew large holes in leaves.
   Control: "Dipel" (Thuricide)—a parasitic bacterium spray.
6. *Fungus gnats*—small, black flies on the medium surface, favored by the presence of moisture. Larvae eat plant roots.
   Control: use yellow, sticky pest strips, pesticides, and keep surface of the growing medium dry.

Sterilization between crops greatly reduces pest and disease problems in the growing medium. Still, aerial parts of the plants are susceptible to them. By maintaining environmental conditions favorable to the plant rather than to the pest, many problems can be avoided.

For example, high humidity favors diseases and some insects. Act quickly to identify the problems and initiate control measures early at the most susceptible stage of the insect's life cycle. This is generally the early infection stage of diseases and the active adult, nymph, or larval stages of feeding insects. Eggs generally are resistant to pesticides.

For successful biological control, you must use only selective pesticides that do not harm useful predators while reducing population outbreaks of the prey. You must maintain predator and prey populations in balance. This is difficult in a small indoor unit; it is easier in a backyard greenhouse, providing that the air inlet louvers and the exhaust fan openings are screened.

You should always check with your local garden center on the safe use of pesticides, and always read and follow the manufacturer's directions and cautions.

The use of a sterile medium in soilless culture reduces pest and disease problems, especially those associated with soil. Maintaining clean beds and sterilizing between crops will significantly depress or eliminate root diseases and pests.

Of course, such problems can easily be introduced if infected

Figure 91. Leaf mold on tomatoes.

Figure 92. Tobacco mosaic virus (TMV) of tomato. Note the distorted leaves of the plant.

Figure 93. Powdery mildew of cucumber.

Figure 94. Two-spotted spider mite damage to cucumber leaves.

Figure 95. Leafminer damage to tomato.

Figure 96. European cucumbers harvested in a plastic tote bin.

Figure 97. Cantaloupe growing vertically in water culture.

plants are transplanted into the hydroponic system. To avoid this, propagate plants from seed in sterile propagation blocks such as peat pellets or rockwool blocks and grow them as seedlings in clean plastic flats or trays. Never set them directly on soil, but place them on a sheet of polyethylene to prevent infection by soil-borne pests. With clean hands, transplant them into the hydroponic system. A little care and cleanliness during propagation and transplanting will prevent potential pest problems.

Weeds are not a problem in soilless culture unless their seeds are introduced. Unlike soil, in which weed seeds are present in large numbers, a sterile medium is free of such seed.

Algae will grow readily in hydroponic systems if light reaches the nutrient solution. Keep all channels, beds, etc., covered. To prevent algal growth on the surface of gravel or sand-culture systems, use drip irrigation lines and do not allow the medium surface to become moist with the nutrient solution.

With a keen interest in gardening, cleanliness, favorable environmental conditions, and proper cultural practices, you will be a very successful hydroponic gardener, providing your family with healthful, flavorful vegetables and fruits (figs. 53–55, 72, 73, 86, 96–99).

The produce, of course, will be but one part of the total enjoyment of growing food hydroponically. This useful hobby will expand your knowledge of the science of horticulture and perhaps lead you to explore new food varieties, or even exotic and ornamental crops (figs. 100–102). Each new hydroponic crop is a stimulating and enjoyable challenge.

Figure 98. European bibb lettuce growing in a raceway system.

Figure 99. Looseleaf lettuce growing in sand culture.

Figure 100. Miniature basil in plastic trough nutrient film technique (NFT) system. *Courtesy of Gourmet Hydro-ponics, Lake Wales, Florida.*

Figure 101. Dish gardens growing tropical foliage plants in a peat medium.

Figure 102. Cacti arrangements growing in sand-peat medium.

Appendix

Note: This is not a complete list of suppliers of these products. The publisher offers without charge a periodically updated list.

Biological Control Agents

Applied Bio-Nomics Ltd.
P.O. Box 2637
Sidney, B.C.
Canada V8L 4C1

Beneficial Bugs
P.O. Box 1627
Apopka, FL 32703-1627

Hydro-Gardens Inc.
P.O. Box 9707
Colorado Springs, CO 80932

Koppert (UK) Ltd.
Biological Control
P.O. Box 43
Tunbridge Wells
Kent TN2 5BX
United Kingdom

Organic Pest Management
P.O. Box 55267
Seattle, WA 98155

Rincon-Vitova Insectories Inc.
P.O. Box 95
Oak View, CA 93022

Hydroponic Consultants & Technology

Agro-Dynamics Inc.
12 Elkins Rd.,
East Brunswick, N.J. 08816

International Aquaponics, Inc.
819 W. 20th Ave.
Vancouver, B.C.
Canada V5Z 1Y3

Hydroponic and Soilless Culture Society

Hydroponics Society of America
P.O. Box 6067
Concord, CA 94524

Hydroponic Equipment & Supplies

Agro-Dynamics, Inc.
12 Elkins Rd.
East Brunswick, N.J. 08816

Agro-Dynamics, Inc.
  Western Division
6492 South Heritage Place E.
Englewood, CO 80111

American Horticultural Supply
25603 West Ave. Stanford
Valencia, CA 91355

Applied Hydroponics, Inc.
3135 Kerner Blvd.
San Rafael, CA 94901

Applied Hydroponics
  of Philadelphia, Inc.
208 Rt. 13
Bristol, PA 19007

Aqua Culture, Inc.
700 W. First St.
Tempe, AZ 85281

Aqua-Ponics
1920 Estes Rd.
Los Angeles, CA 90041

Raymond Bridwell
Box 192
Perris, CA 92370

Brisbon Enterprises
209 Riley Drive
Pacheco, CA 94553

Canadian Hydrogardens Ltd.
411 Brook Rd. West
Ancaster, Ontario
Canada L9G 3L1

Dr. Chatelier's Plant Food
400 Douglas Road East
Oldsmar, FL 34677

Clover Greenhouse by Elliot
P.O. Box 789
Smyrna, TN 37167

CropKing, Inc.
P.O. Box 310
Medina, OH 44258

Dansco Indoor Garden Center
844 University Blvd.
Berkeley, CA 94701

Eco Enterprises
2821 NE 55th St.
Seattle, WA 98105

Electro-Tek of Albuquerque
7504 Dellwood Rd., NE
Albuquerque, NM 87110

Engineered Systems and Designs
3 South Tatnall St.
Wilmington, DE 19801

ENP
200 North Main St.
Mendota, IL 60507

Foothill Hydroponics
10705 Burbank Blvd.
North Hollywood, CA 91601

Full Moon Farm Products
P.O. Box 2046
217 SW 2nd
Corvalis, OR 97339

Genova Products
7034 East Court St.
Davison, MI 48423

Geotechnology
1035 17th Ave.
Santa Cruz, CA 95062

W. R. Grace & Co.
62 Whittemore Ave.
Cambridge, MA 02140

Hollister's Hydroponics
P.O. Box 16601
Irvine, CA 92713

Homegrown, Inc.
12605 Pacific Ave.
Tacoma, WA 98444

Hydro-Gardens, Inc.
P.O. Box 9707
Colorado Springs, CO
80932

Hydro-Harvest Systems
P.O. Box 2590
Homeland, CA 92348

Hydroponic Technologies
1313 Ritchie Ct., Suite 2401
Chicago, IL 60610

Hydro-Tech
3929 Aurora Ave., N
Seattle, WA 98103

The Indoor Gardener
1311 South Pacific Hwy.
Talent, OR 97540

Leisure Garden
P.O. Box 5038
Winston-Salem, NC 27113

Light Mfg. Co.
1634 SE Brooklyn
Portland, OR 97202

Living Green, Inc.
4091 E. La Palma Ave., Suite E
Anaheim, CA 92807

McCalif
2215 Ringwood Ave.
San Jose, CA 95131

J. M. McConkey and Co.
P.O. Box 309
Sumner, WA 98390

Mellinger's
2310 W. South Range Rd.
North Lima, OH 44452

Micro Essential Laboratory
4224 Ave. H
Brooklyn, NY 11210

Midwest Growers Supply
2613 Kaneville Court
Geneva, IL 60134

Nature's Control
P.O. Box 35
Medford, OR 97501

Northwest Seed & Pet
East 2422 Sprague
Spokane, WA 99202

Rambridge Structure and Design
1316 Centre St., NE
Calgary, Alberta T2E 2A7

Reed Company
16714 Meridian St. #239
Puyallup, WA 98373

Rehau Plastics, Inc.
P.O. Box 1706
Leesburg, VA 22075

Reko bv
P.O. Box 191
6190 AD Beek (L)
The Netherlands

Harry Sharp & Son Ltd.
P.O. Box 1918
Renton, WA 98055

Suncor Systems, Inc.
P.O. Box 11116
Portland, OR 97211

Superior Growers Supply
4870 Dawn Ave.
East Lansing, MI 48823

Troy Hygro-Systems, Inc.
4096 Hwy. ES
East Troy, WI 53120

Jack Van Klaveren Ltd. (JVK)
P.O. Box 910
St. Catharines, Ontario
Canada L2R 6Z4

Westbrook Greenhouse Systems
270 Hunter Rd.
Grimsby, Ontario
Canada L3M 5G1

Western Water Farms
2803 Shaughnessy St.
Port Coquitlam, B.C.
Canada V3C 3H1

Westmark Company
3529 Touriga Dr.
Pleasanton, CA 94566

Seeds

De Ruiter Seeds, Inc.
P.O. Box 20228
Columbus, OH 43220

Park Seed Co., Wholesale Div.
736 Cokesbury Rd.
Greenwood, SC 29647

Penn State Seed Co.
Route 309
P.O. Box 390
Dallas, PA 18612

Petoseed Company, Inc.
P.O. Box 4206
Saticoy, CA 93004

Stokes Seeds, Inc.
2103 Stokes Bldg.
Buffalo, NY 14240

Stokes Seeds Ltd.
39 James St., Box 10
St. Catharines, Ontario
Canada L2R 6R6

Vaughan's Seed Co.
5300 Katrine Ave.,
Downers Grove, IL 60515

Scientific Supply Houses

Cole-Parmer Instrument Co.
7425 North Oak Park
Chicago, IL 60648

Fisher Scientific
50 Fadem Rd.
Springfield, NJ 07081

GIBCO Laboratories
3175 Staley Rd.
Grand Island, NY 14072

GIBCO Laboratories
519 Aldo Ave.
Santa Clara, CA 95050

GIBCO Canada
2260A Industrial St.
Burlington, Ontario
Canada L7P 1A1

Hach Company
1313 Border St., Unit 34
Winnipeg, Manitoba
Canada R3H 0X4

Myron L Co.
6231 C Yarrow Dr.,
Carlsbad, CA 92009

Markson
7815 S. 46th St.
Phoenix, AZ 85044-4399

Soil and Plant Tissue Testing Laboratories

Dept. of Land Resource Science
   University of Guelph
Guelph, Ontario, Canada

Griffin Laboratories
1875 Spall Rd.
Kelowna, B.C.
Canada V1Y 4R2

Ohio State University
Ohio Agricultural Research and
   Development Center
Research-Extension Analytical
   Laboratory
Wooster, OH 44691

Soil and Plant Laboratory, Inc.
P.O. Box 11744
Santa Ana, CA 92711

P.O. Box 153
Santa Clara, CA 95052

P.O. Box 1648
Bellevue, WA 98009

Soil Testing Laboratory
Purdue University
Agronomy Dept.
Lafayette, IN 47907

Soil Testing Laboratory
Texas A & M University
College Station, TX 77843

Trade Magazines and Periodicals

American Vegetable Grower
Meister Publ. Co.
Willoughby, OH 44094

Greenhouse Canada
Cash Crop Farming Publ. Ltd.
Delhi, Ontario, Canada

21st Century Gardener
Grower's Press, Inc.
Box 189
Princeton, BC V0X 1W0
Canada

Growing Edge
New Moon Publishing
Box 1027
Corvallis, OR 97339

Greenhouse Grower
Meister Publ. Co.
Willoughby, OH 44094

Greenhouse Manager
Box 1868
Fort Worth, TX 76101

Conversion Factors

	Units	Conversion Factor	Metric Units
Length:	inches	2.54	centimeters
	feet	0.305	meters
	yard	0.915	meters
	miles	1.6	kilometers
	centimeters	0.394	inches
	meters	3.28	feet
	meters	1.094	yards
	kilometers	0.6214	miles
Area:	square inches	6.5	square centimeters
	square feet	0.093	square meters
	acres	0.405	hectares
	square centimeters	0.155	square inches
	square meters	10.76	square feet
	hectares	2.47	acres
Volume:	cubic inches	16.4	cubic centimeters
	cubic feet	0.03	cubic meters
	cubic yards	0.765	cubic meters
	cubic centimeters	0.061	cubic inches
	cubic meters	35.31	cubic feet
	cubic meters	1.31	cubic yards
	U.S. gallons	3.785	liters
	Imp. gallons	4.545	liters
	liters	0.2642	U.S. gallons
	liters	0.220	Imp. gallons
Weight:	ounces (Av.)	28.35	grams
	pounds (Av.)	0.4536	kilograms
	grams	0.0353	ounces (Av.)
	kilograms	2.205	pounds (Av.)
Temperature:	degrees Fahrenheit (F-32)	0.56	degrees Celsius
	degrees Celsius	1.8	degrees Fahrenheit (F + 32)

Examples:

Convert: 8″ to centimeters (cm): $8″ \times 2.54 = 20.32$ cm

Convert: 40°F to Celsius: $(40 - 32) \times 0.56 = 8 \times 0.56 = 4.48$°C

Convert: 10°C to Fahrenheit: $(10 \times 1.8) + 32 = 50$°F

Bibliography

Horticulture

Felton, Elise. 1990. Artistically cultivated herbs. Santa Barbara, Calif.: Woodbridge, Press.

Foster, G. B. and R. F. Louden. 1980. Park's success with herbs. George Park Seed Co., Inc. Greenwood, SC.

Griffin, M. J. and D. V. Alfrod. 1986. Control of pests and diseases of protected crops—Cucumbers. Min. of Agric., Fisheries and Food. ADAS Booklet 2523. London: MAFF Publ.

Jarvis, W. R. and V. W. Nuttall. 1981. Cucumber diseases. Canada Dept. of Agric. Publ. 1684. Agric. Canada, Ottawa, Ontario.

Jarvis. W. R. and C. D. McKenn. 1984. Tomato diseases. Canada Dept. of Agric. Publ. 1479/E. Agric. Canada, Ottawa, Ontario.

Nelson, Paul V. 1985. Greenhouses operation and management. 3rd ed. Reston, Virginia: Reston Publ. Co.

Grower Guide No. 15. Cucumbers, 1983, London: Grower Books.

Golden Nature Guide. Insect Pests. New York: Golden Press.

Golden Science Guide. Botany. New York: Golden Press.

Roorda van Eysinga, J. P. N. L. and K. W. Smilde. 1981. Nutritional disorders in glasshouse tomatoes, cucumbers, and lettuce. Wageningen: Center for Agric. Publ. and Documentation.

Smith, D. 1986. Peppers & aubergines—Grower Guide No. 3. London: Grower Books.

Starr, C. and R. Taggart. 1984. Biology the unity and diversity of life. 3rd ed. Belmont, Calif.: Wadsworth.

Steiner, M. Y. and D. P. Elliott. 1983. Biological pest management for interior plantscapes. Min. of Agric. and Food, Victoria, B.C., Canada.

Wittwer, S. H. and S. Honma. 1979. Greenhouse tomatoes, lettuce, and cucumbers. East Lansing, Michigan: Michigan State Univ. Press.

Hydroponics

Bentley, M. 1974. Hydroponics plus. Sioux Falls, South Dakota: O'Connor Printers.

Bridwell, R. 1990. Hydroponic gardening, rev. ed. Santa Barbara, Calif.: Woodbridge Press.

Cooper, A. J. 1979. The ABC of NFT. London: Grower Books.

Dalton, L. and R. Smith. 1984. Hydroponic gardening. Auckland: Cobb/Horwood Publ.

Douglas, J. S. 1973. Beginner's guide to hydroponics. London: Pelham Books.

Harris, D. 1974. Hydroponics: The gardening without soil. 4th ed. Capetown: Purnell.

Hudson, J. 1975. Hydroponic greenhouse gardening. Garden Grove, Calif.; National Graphics, Inc.

Jones, L. 1977. Home hydroponics . . . and how to do it! Pasadena, Calif.: Ward Ritchie Press.

Kenyon, S. 1979. Hydroponics for the home gardener. Toronto, Ontario: Van Nostrand Reinhold Ltd.

Resh, H. M. 1989. Hydroponic food production. 4th ed. Santa Barbara, Calif.: Woodbridge Press.

Smith, D. L. 1987. Rockwool in horticulture. London: Grower Books.